Woe Is I

The Grammarphobe's Guide to Better English in Plain English

Patricia T. O'Conner

RIVERHEAD BOOKS
A MEMBER OF PENGUIN GROUP (USA) INC.
NEW YORK
2003

For Stewart

Riverhead Books
a member of
Penguin Group (USA) Inc.
375 Hudson Street
New York, NY 10014

Copyright © 1996, 2003 by Patricia T. O'Conner
All rights reserved. This book, or parts thereof, may not
be reproduced in any form without permission.
Published simultaneously in Canada

Library of Congress Cataloging-in-Publication Data

O'Conner, Patricia T.
Woe is I : the grammarphobe's guide to better English in plain English /
Patricia T. O'Conner.
p. cm.
Rev. ed. of: Woe is I. c1996.
Includes bibliographical references and index.
ISBN 1-57322-252-6
1. English language—Grammar—Handbooks, manuals, etc.
2. English language—Usage—Handbooks, manuals, etc.
I. Title: Woe is I.   II. O'Conner, Patricia T. Woe is I.   III. Title.
PE1112.O28   2003   2003041416
428.2—dc21

Printed in the United States of America
1   3   5   7   9   10   8   6   4   2

Book design by Brian Mulligan/Lovedog Studio

Woe Is I

Also by Patricia T. O'Conner

Words Fail Me:
What Everyone Who Writes Should Know About Writing

You Send Me: Getting It Right When You Write Online
(with Stewart Kellerman)

Contents

Preface to the Second Edition

Second editions often make a bashful entrance, pink about the ears and somewhat apologetic. Their very existence, after all, suggests that the original now lacks a certain something. But language books are different. They're expected to grow and change along with languages and the people who use them. And that goes double for books about English, that miracle of flexibility and verbal renewal.

When *Woe Is I* first appeared, English was establishing itself as the global language. Seven years later, it's established. English has become the voice of international business, science, politics, technology, medicine, culture—and, not least, of the Internet. More and more, communicating means communicating in English.

This new edition takes a fresh look at what "better English" is, and isn't, in the twenty-first century. But don't expect any earthshaking changes in what's considered grammatically correct. We don't ditch the rules of grammar and start over every day, or even every generation. The things that make English seem so changeable have more to do with vocabulary and how it's used than with the underlying grammar. And never before have words and usage changed so rapidly, thanks in part to the Internet.

In the age of e-mail, we're continually being called on to alter our notions of what's acceptable and what's not. So *Woe Is I* now includes a chapter about e-mail and other online writing.

Despite the alterations, though, the philosophy of *Woe Is I* remains unchanged. English is a glorious invention, one that gives us endless possibilities for expressing ourselves. Grammar is there to help, to clear up ambiguities and prevent misunderstandings. Any "rule" of grammar that gets in the way or doesn't make sense or creates problems instead of solving them probably isn't a rule at all. (Check out Chapter 9.)

And, as the book's whimsical title hints, it's even possible to be *too* correct. While "Woe is I" may appear technically correct (and that's a matter of opinion), the expression "Woe is me" has been good English for generations. Only a pompous twit—or an author trying to make a point—would use "I" instead of "me" here. As you can see, English is nothing if not reasonable.

Many of the good citizens who were acknowledged in the original *Woe Is I* also made valuable suggestions for the second edition, especially my old friends Charles Doherty and

Tim Sacco. I'm indebted as well to all the readers whose kib-
itzing from the sidelines helped make the book better, particularly David A. Ball, Jason W. Brunk, Liz Copeland, Don
Corken, Jr., Victor Carl Friesen, Mary Laura Gibbs, David
Hawkins, Hunt B. Jones, Anita Kern, Zilia L. Laje, Ruth M.
McVeigh, Ed Pearson, Jessica Raimi, Louie G. Robinson,
James Smith Rudolph, and Scott Summerville. And salaams
to Wendy Carlton and the staff at Riverhead Books for seeing
the new edition into print.

Acknowledgments

Countless friends and colleagues helped make this book by contributing ideas, pointing out omissions, and sneering at my mistakes. I'm glad that I was able to provide you all with a socially acceptable outlet for your more aggressive impulses. Your patience and good humor were second only to mine, and I can't thank you enough.

I'm particularly grateful to those who read the manuscript: Laurie Asséo; David Feldman; Margalit Fox; Elizabeth Frenchman; Anita Gates; Neal, Margo, and Garth Johnston; Dimi Karras; Peter Keepnews; David Kelly; Eden Ross Lipson; Deborah Nye; Allan M. Siegal; Rachel Elkind Tourre; Gloria Gardiner Urban; Elizabeth Weis; and my mother, Beverly J. Newman.

For their support, encouragement, and advice, I thank Michael Anderson; Michael Barson; Alida Becker; Brenda

Berkman; Charles Doherty; Tom Ferrell; Ken Gordon; Pamela and Larry Kellerman; Harvey Kleinman; Charles McGrath; Merrill Perlman; Tim Sacco; Michael Sniffen; Katlyn Stranger; Yves Tourre; Marilynn K. Yee; Arline Youngman; my sister, Kathy Richard; my encyclopedic father-in-law, Allen G. Kellerman; my agent, Dan Green; and Kate Murphy and Anna Jardine at Putnam.

Sam Freedman was generous with his time and advice, and passed along much valuable insight (especially about danglers) from his experiences as a reporter, an author, and a teacher. William Safire was kind enough to acquaint me with the invaluable Jeff McQuain, who expertly scoured the manuscript for errors. (Any boo-boos that remain are mine alone.) And this book couldn't have been written without the help of Jane Isay, whose idea it was in the first place.

Finally, heartfelt thanks to my husband, Stewart Kellerman, for his conjugal as well as conjugational expertise. He put his own book aside many, many times to help me with mine. He's my best friend, and the best editor I know.

Introduction

We all come from the factory wired for language. By the time we know what it is, we've got it. Toddlers don't think about language; they just talk. Grammar is a later addition, an ever-evolving set of rules for using words in ways that we can all agree on. But the laws of grammar come and go. English today isn't what it was a hundred years ago, and it's not what it will be a hundred years from now. We make up rules when we need them, and discard them when we don't. Then when *do* we need them? When our wires get crossed and we fail to understand one another.

If language were flawless, this wouldn't happen, of course. But the perfect language hasn't been invented. No, I take that back—it has been done. There are so-called rational languages (like the "universal" tongue Esperanto and the computer-generated Eliza) that are made up, designed to be logical, reasonable, easy to speak and spell, to make sense. And guess what? They're flat as a pancake. What's missing is the quirkiness, as well as the ambiguity, the bumpy irregularities that make natural languages so exasperating and shifty—and so wonderful. That's wonderful in the literal sense: full of wonders and surprises, poetry and unexpected charm. If English weren't so stretchy and unpredictable, we wouldn't have Lewis Carroll, Dr. Seuss, or the Marx Brothers. And just try telling a knock-knock joke in Latin!

But we pay a price for poetry. English is not easy, as languages go. It began 1,500 years ago, when Germanic tribes (mainly Angles and Saxons) invaded Britain, a Celtic-speaking land already colonized by Latin-speaking Romans. Into this Anglo-Saxon stew went big dollops of French, Italian, Spanish, German, Danish, Portuguese, Dutch, Greek, and more Latin. Within a few hundred years, English was an extraordinarily rich broth. Today, it's believed to have the largest lexicon (that is, the most words) of any modern language—and it's still evolving. Is there any wonder the rules are a little screwy?

And let's face it, English *is* screwy. Bright, educated, technologically savvy people who can run a computer spreadsheet with their toes are heard every day saying things like:

"Come to lunch with the boss and I."

"Somebody forgot their umbrella."

"Already housebroken, the Queen brought home a new corgi."

Every one of those sentences has an outrageous howler (if

you don't see them, check out chapters 1 and 7). Some kinds of flubs have become so common that they're starting to sound right to our ears. And in some cases, they are right. What used to be regarded as errors may now be acceptable or even preferred. What are we supposed to make of all this?

Woe Is I is a survival guide for intelligent people who probably never have diagrammed a sentence and never will. Most of us don't know a gerund from a gerbil and don't care, but we'd like to speak and write as though we did. Grammar is mysterious to each of us in a different way. Some very smart people mess up pronouns, and I've known brilliant souls who can't spell. Many people can't tell the difference between *it's* and *its*. Others go out of their way to avoid using quotation marks. Whatever your particular boo-boo, *Woe Is I* can help you fix it without hitting you over the head with a lot of technical jargon. No heavy lifting, no assembly required. There are sections on the worst pitfalls of everyday language, along with commonsense tips on how to avoid stumbling into them. Wherever possible, I've tried to stay away from grammatical terms, which most of us relish about as much as a vampire does garlic. You don't need them to use English well. If you come across a term that gives you trouble, there's a glossary in the back.

One last word before you plunge in. A dictionary is a wonderful tool, and everybody should have at least one. Yet the fact that a word can be found in the dictionary doesn't make it acceptable English. The job of a dictionary is to describe how words are used at a particular time. Formal or standard meanings are given, but so are colloquial, slang, dialect, sub-standard, regional, and other current meanings. A dictionary may tell you, for example, what's meant by words like "restau-ranteur" and "irregardless" (both, as you'll see, impostors)—but you wouldn't want to embarrass yourself by using them. Buy a standard dictionary (there are recommendations in the bibliography), and read the fine print.

The best of us sometimes get exasperated with the com-plexities of using English well. Believe me, it's worth the ef-fort. Life might be easier if we all spoke Latin. But the quirks, the surprises, the ever-changing nature of English—these are the differences between a living language and a dead one.

Woe Is I

T h e r a p y   f o r
P r o n o u n   A n x i e t y

When a tiny word gives you a big headache, it's probably a pronoun.

Pronouns are usually small (*I, me, he, she, it*), but they're among the biggest troublemakers in the language. If you've ever been picked on by the pronoun police, don't despair. You're in good company. Hundreds of years after the first Ophelia cried "Woe is me," only a pedant would argue that Shakespeare should have written "Woe is I" or "Woe is unto me." (Never mind that the rules of English grammar weren't even formalized in Shakespeare's day.) The point is that no one is exempt from having his pronouns second-guessed.

Put simply, a pronoun is an understudy for a noun. *He* may stand in for "Ralph," *she* for "Alice," *they* for "the Kramdens," and *it* for "the stuffed piranha." Why do we need them? Take the following sentence: *Ralph smuggled his stuffed piranha*

1

into the Kramdens' apartment, sneaked **it** *out of* **his** *jacket, and was slipping* **it** *into* **his** *wife's curio cabinet, when suddenly Alice walked into* **their** *living room, clutched* **her** *heart, and screamed,* "**You** *get* **that** *out of* **my** *house!*"

If no one had invented pronouns, here's how that sentence would look: *Ralph smuggled Ralph's stuffed piranha into the Kramdens' apartment, sneaked the stuffed piranha out of Ralph's jacket, and was slipping the stuffed piranha into Ralph's wife's curio cabinet, when suddenly Alice walked into the Kramdens' living room, clutched Alice's heart, and screamed, "Ralph, get the stuffed piranha out of Alice's house!"*

See how much time pronouns save?

Simple substitutions (like *his* for *Ralph's*) are easy enough. Things get complicated when a pronoun, like any good understudy, takes on different guises, depending on the roles it plays in the sentence. Some pronouns are so well disguised that you may not be able to tell one from another. Enter *that* and *which; it's* and *its; who's* and *whose; who* and *whom; everybody* and *nobody;* and *their, they're,* and *theirs.*

Now let's round up the usual suspects, as well as a few other shady characters.

✳   ✳   ✳

The Which Trials:
That or Which?

Bite on one of these: *Nobody likes a dog **that** bites* or *Nobody likes a dog **which** bites.*

If they both sound right, you've been spooked by *which*es (the first example is the correct one).

The old *that*-versus-*which* problem haunts everybody sooner or later. Here are two rules to help you figure out whether a clause (a group of words with its own subject and verb) should start with *that* or *which.*

- If you can drop the clause and not lose the point of the sentence, use *which*. If you can't, use *that*.
- A *which* clause goes inside commas. A *that* clause doesn't.

Now let's put the rules to work. Look at these two sentences:

*Buster's bulldog, **which** had one white ear, won best in show.*
*The dog **that** won best in show was Buster's bulldog.*

The point of each sentence is that Buster's dog won. What happens when we remove the *that* or *which* clause?

In the first example, the *which* clause (**which** *had one white ear*) is disposable—without it, we still have the gist of the sentence: *Buster's bulldog won best in show.*

But in the second example, the *that* clause (**that** *won best* *in show*) is essential. The sentence misses the point without it: *The dog was Buster's bulldog.*

Some people consider *which* more refined or elegant than *that*. Not so! In fact, *that* is more likely to be grammatically correct than *which*. That's because most of us don't put unessential information in the middle of our sentences, especially when speaking.

Here's a little memory aid:

C o m m a   S e n s e
Commas, *which* cut out the fat,
Go with *which,* never with *that.*

An Itsy-Bitsy Problem: It's or Its?

The smaller the word, the handier it is. And *it* is about as useful as they come. *It* can stand in for anything—a stuffed piranha, existentialism, the Monroe Doctrine, or buttered toast. It's a very versatile pronoun! But did you notice what just happened? We added an *s* and got *it's*—or should that be *its*? Hmmm. When do you use *it's,* and when do you use *its*?

This is an itsy-bitsy problem that gives lots of intelligent people fits. They go wrong when they assume that a word with an apostrophe must be a possessive, like *Bertie's aunt.* But an apostrophe can also stand for something that's been omitted (as in contractions, which are run-together words like *can't* and *shouldn't*). In this case, *it's* is short for *it is*. Plain *its* is the possessive form. So here's the one and only rule you need:

- If you can substitute *it is,* use *it's.*

NOTE: *It's* can also be short for *it has*. There's more on *its* versus *it's* in the chapter on possessives, page 39.

Who's (or Whose) on First?

This problem is a first cousin of the one above (which you should look at, if you haven't already). As with *it's* and *its,* remember that *who's* is shorthand for *who is,* and unadorned *whose* is the possessive form.

- If you can substitute *who is,* use *who's.*

NOTE: *Who's* can also be short for *who has*. There's more on *whose* versus *who's* in the chapter on possessives, page 40.

You're on Your Own

"Your our kind of people," reads the hotel marquee. Eek! Let's hope impressionable children aren't looking. The sign should

Who's That?

Choose one: *The girl* **that** *married dear old dad* or *The girl* **who** *married dear old dad.*

If both sound right, it's because both are right.

A person can be either a *that* or a *who.* A thing, on the other hand, is always a *that.*

But what about Benjy and Morris? Dogs and cats aren't people, but they aren't quite things, either. Is an animal a *that* or a *who*?

If the animal is anonymous, it's a *that: There's the dog* **that** *won the Frisbee competition.*

If the animal has a name, he or she can be either a *who* or a *that: Morris is a cat* **who** *knows what he likes.*

read: "You're our kind of people." *You're* is short for *you are*; *your* is the possessive form.

- If you can substitute *you are,* use *you're.*

Whom Sweet Whom

Poor *whom*! Over the years, wordsmiths from Noah Webster to Jacques Barzun have suggested that maybe we should ditch it altogether and let *who* do the job of both. Not a bad idea. It's pretty hard to imagine an outraged populace protesting, "*Whom* do you think you're messing with! Get your hands off our pronouns!" There's no doubt that in everyday speech, *whom* has lost the battle.

So has the bell tolled for *whom*?

Not quite. Here we are, well into a new millennium, and against all odds, creaky old *whom* is still with us. With a few minor adjustments, we can get away with dropping it when we speak (I'll show you how on page 9), though even that may raise an eyebrow or two. But since written English is more formal than conversational English, anyone who wants to write correctly will have to get a grip on *whom*.

If you want to be absolutely correct, the most important thing to know is that *who* does something (it's a subject, like *he*), and *whom* has something done to it (it's an object, like *him*). You might even try mentally substituting *he* or *him* where *who* or *whom* should go: if *him* fits, you want *whom* (both end in *m*); if *he* fits, you want *who* (both end in a vowel). *Who* does something *to* (*at, by, for, from, in, toward, upon, with,* etc.) *whom*. The words in parentheses, by the way, are prepositions, words that "position"—that is, locate—other words. A preposition often comes just before *whom*, but not always. A better way to decide between *who* and *whom* is to ask yourself *who* is doing what to *whom*.

This may take a little detective work. Miss Marple herself might have been stumped by the convolutions of some *who* or *whom* clauses (a clause, you'll recall, is a group of words with its own subject and verb). For instance, other words may get in between the subject and the verb. Or the object may end up in front of both the subject and the verb. Here are two pointers to help clear up the mystery, and examples of how they're used.

- Simplify, simplify, simplify: strip the clause down to its basic subject, verb, and object.
- Move the words around mentally to make it easier to identify the subject and the object.

*Nathan invited only guys [**who** or **whom**] he thought played for high stakes.* If you strip the clause of its false clues—the words separating the subject and verb—you' end up with *who . . . played for high stakes.* *Who* did something (played for high stakes), so it's the subject.

*Nathan wouldn't tell Miss Adelaide [**who** or **whom**] he invited to his crap game.* First strip the sentence down to the basic clause, *[**who** or **whom**] he invited.* If it's still unclear, rearrange the words in your mind: *he invited **whom**.* You can now see that *whom* is the object—*he* did something to (invited) *whom*—even though *whom* comes ahead of both the verb and the subject.

NOTE: A preposition isn't necessarily followed by *whom.* It can be followed by a clause that starts with *who.* Consider this sentence: *After the crap game, Nathan was confused about [**who** or **whom**] owed him money.* Don't be misled by the preposition *about;* it's one of the

A Cure for the Whom-Sick

Now for the good news. In almost all cases, you can use *who* instead of *whom* in conversation or in informal writing, like personal letters and casual memos.

Sure, it's not a hundred percent correct, and I don't recommend using it on the most formal occasions, but *who* is certainly less stuffy, especially at the beginning of a sentence or a clause: **Who***'s the letter from? Did I tell you* **who** *I saw at the movies?* **Who** *are you waiting to see? No matter* **who** *you invite, someone will be left out.*

A note of caution: *Who* can sound grating if used for *whom* right after a preposition. You can get around this by putting *who* in front. *From* **whom**? becomes **Who** *from*? So when a colleague tells you he's going on a Caribbean cruise and you ask, "Who with?" he's more likely to question your discretion than your grammar.

false clues mentioned above. Instead, simplify, simplify, simplify, and look for the clause—in this case it's *who owed him money.* Since *who* did something (owed him money), it's the subject.

Object Lessons

The *Me* Generation

These days, anyone who says "It is I" sounds like a stuffed shirt. It wasn't always so. In bygone days, you might have had your knuckles rapped for saying "It's me" instead of "It is I." Your crime? A pronoun following the verb *to be,* the English teacher insisted, should act like a subject (*I, he, she, they*) and not an object (*me, him, her, them*). But language is a living thing, always evolving, and *It is I* is just about extinct. In all but the most formal writing, some of the fussiest grammarians accept *It's me.* Most of us find the old usage awkward, though I must admit that I still use "This is she" when someone asks for me on the phone. Old habits die harder than old rules.

Next time you identify the perp in a police lineup, feel free to point dramatically and say, "That's him, Officer!"

JUST BETWEEN *ME* AND *I*

Why is it that no one ever makes a mistake like this? *You'll be hearing from I*.

It's instinctive to use the correct form (*from **me***) when only a solitary pronoun follows a preposition. (Prepositions—*after, as, at, before, between, by, for, from, in, like, on, toward, upon, with,* and a slew of others—position other words in the sentence.) But when the pronoun isn't alone, instinct goes down the drain, and grammar with it. So we run into abominations like *The odds were **against you and I***, although no one would dream of saying "against I."

I wouldn't be at all surprised to learn that the seeds of the *I*-versus-*me* problem are planted in early childhood. We're admonished to say, "I want a cookie," not "Me want a cookie." We begin to feel subconsciously that *I* is somehow more genteel than *me,* even in cases where *me* is the right choice—for instance, after a preposition. Trying too hard to be right, we end up being wrong. Hypercorrectness rears its ugly head!

My guess is that most people who make this mistake do so out of habit, without thinking, and not because they don't know the difference between *I* and *me*. If you find yourself automatically putting *you and I* after a preposition, try this: In your mind, eliminate the other guy, leaving the tricky pronoun (*I* or *me*) all by itself. Between you and me, it works.

> **NOTE:** I can hear a chorus of voices shouting, Wait a minute! Doesn't Shakespeare use *I* after a preposition in *The Merchant of Venice?* Antonio tells Bassanio, "All

debts are clear'd between you and I, if I might but see you at my death." That's true. But then, we're not Shakespeare.

More Than Meets the I

Some of the smartest people I know hesitate at the word *than* when it comes before a pronoun. What goes next, *I* or *me? he* or *him? she* or *her? they* or *them?*

The answer: All of the above! This is easier than it sounds. Take *I* and *me* as examples, since they're the pronouns we use most (egotists that we are). Either one may be correct after *than,* depending on the meaning of the sentence.

- *Trixie loves spaghetti* **more than** *I* means **more than** *I do.*
- *Trixie loves spaghetti* **more than** *me* means **more than** *she loves me.*

NOTE: If ending a sentence with *than I* or *than she* or *than they* seems awkward or fussy (particularly in speaking), you might simply add the missing thought: *Harry smokes more* **than they do.**

The Sins of
the Self-ish

In the contest between *I* and *me*, the booby prize often goes to *myself*.

That's why we see sentences like *Jack and **myself** were married yesterday*. (It's *Jack and **I***.) Or like this more common *self*-promotion: *The project made money for Reynaldo and **myself***. The speaker isn't sure whether it's *Reynaldo and **me*** or *Reynaldo and **I***, so she goes with *Reynaldo and **myself***. Tsk, tsk. (It's *for Reynaldo and **me***.)

Myself and the rest of the *self*-ish crew (*yourself, himself, herself, itself, ourselves, yourselves, themselves*) shouldn't take the place of the ordinary pronouns *I* and *me*, *she* and *her*, and so on. They are used for only two purposes:

- To emphasize. *I made the cake **myself**. Love **itself** is a riddle. The detective **himself** was the murderer.* (The emphasis could be left out, and the sentence would still make sense.)

- To refer to the subject. *She hates **herself**. And you call **yourself** a plumber! They consider **themselves** lucky to be alive. The problem practically solved **itself**.*

They and Company:
They're, Their, Theirs
(and There and There's)

These words remind me of the stateroom scene in the Marx Brothers movie *A Night at the Opera*. There seem to be half a dozen too many, all stepping on one another's feet.

Taken one at a time, though, they're pretty harmless.

- *They're* is shorthand for *they are*: **They're** *tightwads, and they always have been.*
- *Their* and *theirs* are the possessive forms for *they*: **Their** *money is* **theirs** *alone.*
- *There* (meaning "in or at that place," as opposed to "here") isn't even a pronoun, unlike the rest of the crowd in the stateroom. Neither is *there's,* which is shorthand for *there is.* But *there* and *there's* frequently get mixed up with the sound-alikes *they're, their,* and *theirs.*

Sometimes a limerick says it best:

The Dinner Guests

They seem to have taken on airs.
They're ever so rude with *their* stares.
They get *there* quite late,
There's a hand in your plate,
And *they're* eating what's not even *theirs.*

How Many Is Everybody?

This may seem like a silly question, but what's wrong with saying, *Are everybody happy?* After all, when you use the word *everybody,* you're thinking of a crowd, right? Then why do we say, *Is everybody happy?*

In other words, just how many people do we mean when we say *everybody* or *everyone?*

The answer is one. Odd as it may seem, these pronouns are singular. We often use them when talking about whole gangs of people, but we treat them grammatically as individual gang members. The result is that each takes a singular verb: *Everybody loves a lover, but not everybody is one.*

There's No Their There

A lot of people start seeing double when they use *anybody, anyone, everybody, everyone, nobody, no one, somebody, someone, each, either,* and *neither.*

Actually, each of these pronouns is singular—yes, even *everybody* and *everyone* (if you have doubts, see the item above). Then why do so many people use the plurals *they, them, their,* and *theirs* as stand-ins? *Somebody forgot **their** coat. If anyone calls, tell **them** I'm out.* I cringe when I hear things like that.

Stick to singular stand-ins (*he, she, it, his, her, hers,* or *its*) for singular pronouns like *everybody* and company: *Somebody forgot **her** coat. If anyone calls, tell **him** I'm out.* You may be tempted to use *their* and *them* because you don't know whether the somebody is a he or a she. Well, your nonsexist intentions are good, but your grammar isn't.

Frankly, this is one of the few times when English lets us down. The only unisex singular pronoun we have is *it,* which doesn't always fill the bill. Since time immemorial, English speakers have used the masculine *he* and *him* and *his* to refer to a person in general. Understandably, some people can't help thinking of those as . . . well . . . male.

If you can't bring yourself to use the all-purpose masculine and you hate the clunky *him or her* alternatives, don't resort to *they* and company. Bad English isn't the answer. My advice is to reword the sentence: *Somebody forgot a coat. If anyone calls, say I'm out.*

When you do use the stand-ins, though, get them right. Here are some examples. If they sound odd, that's because you're used to making mistakes. Join the club.

*Has **anybody** lost **her** purse?* Not: **their** *purse.*

*If **anyone** makes trouble, throw **him** out.* Not: throw **them** *out.*

*Everybody has **his** priorities.* Not: **their** *priorities.*

*Everyone seems happy with **his or her** partner.* Not: **their** *partner.*

*Nobody works overtime because **she** likes it.* Not: **they** *like it.*

No one appreciates *her* husband. Not: *their* husband.

Somebody must have *his* head screwed on backward. Not: *their* head.

Someone has locked *himself* out. Not: *themselves* or (even worse!) *themself*.

Each has *its* drawbacks. Not: *their* drawbacks.

Either has earned *his* stripes. Not: *their* stripes.

Neither was wearing *his* earring. Not: *their* earring.

NOTE: *Either* and *neither* can sometimes be plural when paired with *or* or *nor*. For more, see page 52.

What's What?

Which sentence is correct?

*Lou sees **what appears** to be ghosts* or *Lou sees **what appear** to be ghosts*.

Leaving aside the issue of Lou's sanity, should we choose *what appears* or *what appear*? And what difference does it make? Well, what we're really asking is whether the pronoun *what,* when used as a subject, takes a singular verb (*appears*) or a plural one (*appear*). The answer is that *what* can be either singular or plural; it can mean "the thing that" or "things that." In this case, Lou is seeing "things that" appear to be ghosts. So this is the correct sentence: *Lou sees **what appear** to be ghosts*.

NOTE: When *what* is the subject of two verbs in the same sentence, make the verbs match in number—both singular or both plural, not one of each. ***What** scares Lou the most **is** Bud's sudden disappearance.* (Both verbs are singular.) *But **what seem** to be supernatural events **are** really sleight-of-hand.* (Both verbs are plural.)

By the way, it takes a certain effort to get your *what*s straight. Few people do it automatically, so take your time and watch out for trapdoors. For more on *what* with verbs, see page 54.

Chapter 2

Plurals Before Swine

Blunders with Numbers

With grammar, it's always something. If it's not one thing, it's two—or four, or eight—and that's where plurals come in. Without plural words, we'd have to talk about one thing at a time! You couldn't eat a bag of *peanuts* at the ball game, you'd have to eat *peanut* after *peanut* after *peanut*. But language is very accommodating. A *bagful* here and a *bagful* there and—voilà—you've got *bagfuls*. See? There's nothing we can't have more of, even *infinities*, because anything that can be singular can also be plural.

What Noah Knew

The ark was filled symmetrically:
For every boy, a girl.
Its claim to singularity
Resided in the plural.

In English, it's fairly easy to go forth and multiply. To make a singular noun (a word for a thing, person, place, or idea) into a plural one, we usually add *s* or *es* or *ies,* depending on its ending. In general, plurals are a piece (or pieces) of cake.

Of course, there are dozens of irregular plurals, but most of them are second nature to us by the time we're five or six. *Children* (not "childs") shouldn't play with *knives* (not "knifes"), and ganders are male *geese* (not "gooses"). A little later in life we pick up some of the more exotic plurals—*criteria, phenomena, tableaux,* and the like—that are the off-spring of other languages.

For most of us, plurals get sticky mainly when they involve proper names, nouns with several parts, or words that can be either singular or plural. How do we refer to more than one *Sanchez* or *spoonful* or *brother-in-law*? Is a word like *couple* or *politics* singular or plural—or can it be both?

To get right to the points, let's start with names.

✳   ✳   ✳

Keeping Up
with the Joneses:
How Names Multiply

It baffles me why people mangle names almost beyond recognition when they make them plural. *In my daughter's preschool class, there are two **Larries** [ouch!], three **Jennifer's** [oof!], and two **Sanchez'** [yipes!].* It's *Larrys, Jennifers,* and *Sanchezes.*

Getting it right isn't that difficult. Whether you're dealing with a first name or a last, form the plural by adding *s,* or (if the name ends in *s, sh, ch, x,* or *z*) by adding *es.* A final *y* doesn't change to *ies* at the end of a name. And please, no apostrophes!

*Charles and his friend Charles are just a couple of **Charleses**.*

*When Eliza dated three guys named Henry, she couldn't keep her **Henrys** straight. What's more, two of them were **Higginses**.*

*There are eight **Joneses**, two of them **Marys**, in Reggie's little black book.*

*The **Ricardos** and the **Mertzes** had dinner with the **Simpsons** and the **Flanderses** at the home of the **Cleavers**.*

Compound Fractures:
Words That Come Apart

Some nouns aren't simple; they're more like small construction projects. When a *spoon* is *full,* it's a *spoonful*—but are
two of them *spoonsful* or *spoonfuls*? If your better half has two
brothers, are they your *brothers-in-law* or your *brother-in-
laws*? In other words, how do you make a plural of a noun
with several parts? The answer, as it turns out, comes in
parts:

- If a compound word is solid and has no hyphen (-),
put the normal plural ending at the *end* of the word:

    Churchmen love **soapboxes**.

    Kipling appeals to **schoolchildren** *and* **fishwives**.

    Doormen *are good at getting* **taxicabs**.

    You hardly ever come across Biedermeier **bookcases** *in
    alleyways*.

    Babies dump **spoonfuls** *of jam on* **footstools**.

- If the word is split into parts, with or without hyphens, put the plural ending on the root or most important part (underlined in the examples):

    <u>**Mothers**</u>**-in-law** *like to attend* <u>**courts**</u>**-martial**.

    Are they <u>**ladies**</u>**-in-waiting** *or just* <u>**hangers**</u>**-on**?

    Those <u>**counselors**</u>**-at-law** *ate all the* <u>**crêpes**</u> *suzette*.

    Garter <u>**belts**</u> *aren't required on* <u>**men**</u>**-of-war**.

- Watch out for *general* when it's part of a compound word. In a military title, *general* is usually the important part, so it gets the *s*. In a civilian title, *general* isn't the root, so it doesn't get the *s*:

   Two **attorneys** *general went dancing with two* **major generals**.

   Those **consuls** *general are retired* **brigadier generals**.

The ics Files

Figuring out the mathematics of a noun can be tricky. Take the word *mathematics*. Is it singular or plural? And what about all those other words ending in *ics*—*economics, ethics, optics, politics,* and so on? Fortunately, it doesn't take a Ph.D. in mathematics to solve this puzzle.

If you're using an *ics* word in a general way (as a branch of study, say), it's singular. If you're using an *ics* word in a particular way (as someone's set of beliefs, for example), it's plural.

*"**Politics** stinks," said Mulder.*

*"Mulder's **politics** stink," said Scully.*

***Statistics** isn't a popular course at the academy.*

*Alien-abduction **statistics** are scarce.*

Ifs, Ands, or Buts

In English, there are exceptions to every rule. When *man* or *woman* is part of a compound, often both parts become plural. For example, *man-servant* becomes *menservants; woman doctor* becomes *women doctors; gentleman farmer* becomes *gentlemen farmers.* Two other exceptions to the rules for making compound words plural make no sense at all: *hotfoot* becomes *hotfoots* (believe it or not), and *still life* becomes *still lifes.* Go figure.

On occasion you may need to form a plural of a word like *yes, no,* or *maybe.* Well, since you're referring to them as nouns, just follow the normal rules for making nouns into plurals:

WORDS TO THE WHYS

Ups and downs and ins and outs,
Forevers and nevers and whys.
Befores and afters, dos and don'ts,
Farewells and hellos and good-byes.
Life is a string of perhapses,
A medley of whens and so whats.
We rise on our yeses and maybes,
Then fall on our nos and our buts.

Two-Faced Words: Sometimes Singular, Sometimes Plural

A noun can be double trouble if it stands for a collection of things. Sometimes it's singular and sometimes it's plural. How do you know which is which? Amazingly, common sense (yes, it does have a place in English usage!) should tell you. Ask yourself this question: Am I thinking of the baseball team, or the players? Let's take a swing at these problem words a few at a time.

COUNSELING FOR COUPLES

What is a *couple,* anyway? Is it a pair (singular), or two of a kind (plural)? Is it two peas (plural) in a pod, or a pod (singular) with two peas?

Couple is probably the most common of the two-faced words. It can be either singular or plural, depending on whether it's supposed to mean two individuals or a package deal. Ask yourself whether you have the two peas in mind, or the pod. Here's a hint: Look at the word (*a* or *the*) in front. *The couple* is usually singular. *A couple,* especially when followed by *of,* is usually plural. Each of these examples illustrates both uses (the verbs are underlined, one plural and one singular):

A **couple** of tenants <u>own</u> geckos. The **couple** in 5G <u>owns</u> a family of mongooses.

*Only a **couple** of appointments <u>are</u> available. That **couple** <u>is</u> always late.*

There's more about *couple* in the chapter on verbs; see page 53.

Group Therapy

Many words that mean a group of things—*total, majority,* and *number,* for example—can be singular or plural. Sometimes they mean the group acting as a whole, sometimes the members of the group.

As with the other two-faced words, ask yourself whether you are thinking of the whole or the parts. A little hint: *The* before the word (*the total, the majority*) is usually a tip-off that it's singular, while *a* (*a total, a number*), especially when *of* comes after, usually indicates a plural. Each of these examples illustrates both (the verbs are underlined, one singular and one plural):

*The **majority** <u>is</u> in charge. Still, a **majority** of voters <u>are</u> unhappy.*

*The **total** <u>was</u> in the millions. A **total** of six <u>were</u> missing.*

*The **number** of hats Bette owns is astounding. A **number** of them <u>are</u> pretty ridiculous.*

There's more about *total, majority,* and *number* in the chapter on verbs, page 53.

ALL OR NOTHING

All is a versatile word. It's all things to all people; in fact, it's all-encompassing. So all-inclusive is this little word that it can be either singular or plural. Another two-faced word!

Luckily, it's all too simple to decide whether *all* is singular or plural. Here's a foolproof way (the verbs in the examples are underlined):

- If *all* means "all of it" or "everything" or "the only thing," it's singular: "***All** I eat <u>is</u> lettuce,*" said Kate. "*But **all** I lose <u>is</u> brain cells. **All** <u>is</u> not well with my waist.*"
- If *all* indicates "all of them," it's plural. "***All** the men I date <u>are</u> confused,*" said Kate. "***All** <u>prefer</u> slender women with big appetites.*"

NOTE: The same logic holds for *any*. If it means "any of it," it's singular; if it means "any of them," it's plural. There's more about *any* and *all* in the chapter on verbs, page 53.

NONE SENSE

None is the most difficult of the two-faced words, those that can be either singular or plural. One reason it's so confusing is that generations of us were taught (incorrectly) as schoolchildren that *none* is always singular because it means "not one." Legions of people think of rather stiff sentences—***None** of Dempsey's teeth <u>was</u> chipped*, or ***None** of Tunney's fingers <u>was</u> broken*—as grammatically correct.

But *none* has always been closer in meaning to "not any," and most authorities agree it's usually plural: ***None** of Tyson's teeth were chipped*. ***None** of Holyfield's fingers were broken*. *None* is singular only when it means "none of it" (that is to say, "no amount"): ***None** of the referee's blood was shed*.

Here's an easy way to decide whether *none* is singular or plural (the verbs are underlined):

- If it suggests "none of them," it's plural: ***None** of the fans are fighting*. ***None** are excited enough*.
- If it means "none of it," it's singular: ***None** of the bout was seen in Pittsburgh*. ***None** was worth broadcasting*.

   NOTE: When you really do mean "not one," it's better to say "not one," and use a singular verb: ***Not one** of Holyfield's fingers was broken*.

Y's and Wherefores: Words That End in Y

Some plurals are just a bowl of cherries. Words ending in *y* either add *s* or change the *y* to *ies*. Here's the scoop.

- If a word ends in *y* preceded by a consonant (a hard sound, like *b, d, l, r, t,* etc.), drop the *y* and add *ies*: ***Ladies** don't throw **panties** off the decks of **ferries***.

- If a word ends in *y* preceded by a vowel (a soft, open-mouthed sound, like *a, e, o, u*), add *s*: **Boys** *born in* **alleys** *can grow up to be* **attorneys**.

For making plurals out of names that end in *y*, see page 21.

One Potato, Two Potato: Words That End in O

O for a simple solution to this one! Unfortunately, there's no hard-and-fast rule that tells you how to form the plural of every word that ends in *o*.

- Most form their plurals by adding *s*: **Romeos** *who wear* **tattoos** *and invite* **bimbos** *to their* **studios** *to see their* **portfolios** *are likely to be* **gigolos**.
- A small number of words that end in *o* form their plurals by adding *es*. Some of the most common are in this example: *The* **heroes** *saved the* **cargoes** *of* **tomatoes** *and* **potatoes** *from the* **mosquitoes** *and* **tornadoes** *by hiding them in* **grottoes**.

If you're unsure about the plural of an *o* word, look it up in the dictionary. And if two plurals are given, the one that's listed first is the preferred spelling.

Plurals on the Q.T.: Abbreviations, Letters, and Numbers

No two authorities seem to agree on how we should form the plurals of abbreviations (*GI, rpm, RBI*), letters (*x, y, z*), and numbers (*9, 10*). Should we add *s*, or *'s*? Where one style maven sees *UFO's*, another sees *UFOs*. One is nostalgic for the *1950's*, the other for the *1950s*. This is more a matter of taste and readability than of grammar, and frankly, we have better things to worry about. For the sake of consistency and common sense, here's what I recommend. To form the plurals of all numbers, letters, and abbreviations (with or without periods and capitals), simply add *'s*.

CPA's, those folks who can add columns of 9's in their heads, have been advising MD's since the 1980's to dot their i's, cross their t's, and never accept IOU's. Things could be worse: there could be two IRS's.

Still not convinced? Just try making a plural of the lowercase letter *a* (or *i* or *u* or *s*, among others) without an apostrophe.

Between and From: The Numbers Game

OK, it's not something that's been keeping you awake nights. But it comes up all the time. The question: When a noun follows *between* or *from*, is it singular or plural? *The elevator stalled between the ninth and tenth [floor or floors], stranding the boss from the first to the third [week or weeks] in August.* See what I mean? A small problem, perhaps, but a common one.

The answer: *Between* is followed by a plural noun, and *from* is followed by a singular one: *The elevator stalled between the ninth and tenth floors, stranding the boss from the first to the third week in August.*

Another pair of examples:

Veronica said she lost her charm bracelet somewhere between Thirty-third and Thirty-seventh streets. Archie searched every inch of pavement from Thirty-third to Thirty-seventh Street before realizing that she had been in a cab at the time.

The Soul of Kindness: All Kinds, Sorts, and Types

You've probably heard sentences like this one: *I hate these kind of mistakes!* If it sounds wrong to you, you're right. It's *these kinds of mistakes* (or *that kind of mistake*).

The singulars—*kind* of, *sort* of, *type* of, and *style* of—are preceded by *this* or *that,* and are followed by singular nouns: *Dagwood wears this kind of hat.*

The plurals—*kinds* of, *sorts* of, *types* of, and *styles* of—are preceded by *these* or *those,* and are usually followed by plural nouns: *Mr. Dithers hates those kinds of hats.*

Here are some more examples to help you sort things out:

"*I enjoy **this sort of cigar**,*" *said Dagwood.*

"***These sorts of cigars** disgust me,*" *said Mr. Dithers.*

"***That type of car** is my ideal,*" *said Dagwood.*

"*Only gangsters drive **those types of cars**,*" *said Mr. Dithers.*

Never use *a* or *an* after the expressions *kind of, sort of, type of,* or *variety of: The beagle is some **kind of a** hound.* (Arf!)

> **NOTE:** Some singular nouns can stand for just one thing (*Is the **meat** done?*) or a whole class of things (*The butcher sells many varieties of **meat***). Other singular nouns always stand for a set of things (*The **china** matches the **furniture***). When a singular noun stands for a group of things, it's all right (though not necessary) to use it with *those kinds, these sorts,* and so on. ***Those kinds of china** break easily.* This can be a subtle distinction. If you find it hard to make, you're safer sticking to the all-singular or all-plural rule (*this kind of china*).

Some Things Never Change

You're already familiar with nouns from the animal kingdom that can stand for one critter or many: *fish, deer, moose, vermin, elk, sheep, swine.* Well, some words ending in *s* are also the same in singular and plural: *series, species,* and *headquar-*

ters, which can mean a base or bases: *Gizmo's* **headquarters** *was designed by Rube Goldberg. The rival companies'* **head-quarters** *were on opposite sides of town.*

Looks Can Be Deceiving

Loads of nouns look plural because they end in *s,* but they're actually singular: *checkers* (also *billiards, dominoes,* and other names of games); *measles* (also *mumps, rickets, shingles,* and many other diseases); *molasses; news;* and *whereabouts. Basil says* **checkers** *takes Sybil's mind off her* **shingles,** *which is driving her nuts.*

If that's not confusing enough, how about this? Some nouns that end in *s* and are regarded as pairs—*scissors, trousers, tongs, pliers, tweezers,* and *breeches,* for instance— are singular but treated as plural. *The* **scissors** *were found, as were the* **tweezers,** *in the drawer where the* **pliers** *are kept.*

> **NOTE:** Some words are often used as singular (*data, media*), though for years the traditional meaning has been plural. The ground has shifted here, so for the scoop on such words, see page 184. And if you want a little thrill—all right, I said a *little* thrill—look up *kudos* (singular or plural?) on page 112.

Plurals
with Foreign Accents

A Californian I know, Dr. Schwartz, is a cactus fancier. Is his garden filled with *cactuses* . . . or *cacti?*

As most dictionaries will tell you, either form is right. *Cacti* may sound more exotic, but it's not more correct; in fact, many American dictionaries favor *cactuses.*

As for other nouns of foreign origin, how do you know whether to choose an Anglicized plural (like *memorandums*) or a foreign one (*memoranda*)? There's no single answer, unfortunately. A century ago, the foreign ending would have been preferred, but over the years we've given Anglicized plural endings to more and more foreign-derived words. When you have a choice, take the plural that's listed first in the dictionary.

Here's a partial list of current preferences.

Anglicized: *antennas* (except those on insects), *appendixes, beaus, cactuses, châteaus, curriculums, dictums, formulas, gymnasiums, indexes, memorandums, millenniums, referendums, stadiums, syllabuses, symposiums, ultimatums, virtuosos.*

Multiple Mollusks

In the oceans, wriggling by,

Are *octopuses,* not *octopi.*

Foreign: *analyses, antennae* (on insects), *addenda, algae, axes* (for *axis*), *bacteria, bases* (for *basis*), *crises, criteria, fungi, hypotheses, kibbutzim, larvae, oases, parentheses, phenomena, radii* (but *radiuses* is on the rise), *stimuli, strata, tableaux* (*tableaus* is gaining fast), *theses, vertebrae.*

Plurals can be singularly interesting. Take the octopus—a remarkable creature, grammatically as well as biologically. *Octopus* is from the Greek and means "eight-footed." The original plural was *octopodes,* Anglicized over the years to *octopuses.* Along the way, someone substituted the Latin ending *pi* for the Greek *podes* and came up with the polyglot *octopi.* Though it's technically incorrect, *octopi* is now so common that dictionaries list it as a second choice after *octopuses,* the preferred plural. *Octopi* is for suckers.

Chapter 3

Yours Truly

The Possessives and the Possessed

For an acquisitive society, we're awfully careless about possessives. Have you ever driven through a vacation community and noticed the offhanded signs identifying the properties? *The Miller's, The Davis', The Jone's, Bobs Place.* Businesses are no better, imagining possessives where there aren't any. A now defunct theater near Times Square in New York called itself *The Ero's.* We've all seen places like *Harrys Muffler Shop* or *Glorias' House of Beauty* or *His' and Hers' Formal Wear.*

The word *its* is an Excedrin headache, a possessive that does not take the apostrophe (') we've come to expect. There are scores of other possessive puzzles: Are you a friend *of Jake,* or a friend *of Jake's?* Are you going to your *aunt and uncle's* house, or to your *aunt's and uncle's* house? Do you mind *me smoking,* or do you mind *my smoking?*

As long as there are haves and have-nots, there will be questions about possessives. This chapter should answer the most troublesome ones.

Possession Is Not Demonic: The Simple Facts

The tool kit couldn't be simpler. All you need to make almost any word possessive is an apostrophe and the letter *s*. You add both of them together (*'s*) or just the apostrophe alone, depending on the circumstances:

- If the word is singular, always add *'s*, regardless of its ending. (This is true even if the ending is *s*, *z*, or *x*— whether sounded or silent.) *The waiter spilled red wine on **Eula's** dress, which came from **Paris's** finest shop. The **dress's** skirt, which resembled a tutu from one of **Degas's** paintings, was ruined. **Flem's** attitude was philosophical because he had been reading **Camus's** essays. "It wasn't **Jacques's** fault," he said, defending the waiter. "Besides, it's not this **Bordeaux's** best vintage."*
- If the word is plural and doesn't already end in *s*, add *'s*: *The **children's** menu was a rip-off, and the **men's** room was painted fuchsia.*
- If the word is plural and ends in *s*, add just the apostrophe: *The **Snopeses'** car was stolen by the valet parking*

attendant. *The **cops'** attitude was surly. The **victims'** evening was now demolished.*

And by the way, when you need a comma or a period after a possessive word that ends with an apostrophe, the comma or period goes after the apostrophe and not inside it: *The idea was the **girls'**, or maybe the **boys'**, but at any rate the responsibility was their **parents'**.*

NOTE: Be sure you've formed the plural correctly before you add the apostrophe to the end. There's more about plural names in the chapter on plurals, page 21. In a nutshell, if a name ends in *s* (like *Snopes*) the plural adds *es* (the *Snopeses*) and the plural possessive adds *es'* (the *Snopeses'* car). For a name that doesn't end in an *s* sound (*Babbitt*), the plural adds *s* (the *Babbitts*) and the plural possessive adds *s'* (the *Babbitts'* car).

Its (or It's?): Public Enemy Number 1

What a difference an apostrophe makes. Every possessive has one, right? Well, not necessarily so. *It* (like *he* and *she*) is a pronoun—a stand-in for a noun—and pronouns don't have apostrophes when they're possessives: *His coat is too loud because of **its** color, but **hers** is too mousy.*

Now, as for *it's* (the one with the punctuation), the apostrophe stands for something that has been removed. *It's* is short for *it is,* and the apostrophe replaces the missing *i* in *is. The parakeet is screeching because **it's** time to feed him.*

Here's how to keep *its* and *it's* straight:

- If the word you want could be replaced by *it is,* you want *it's.* If not, use *its.* (There's more on *its* and *it's* in the chapter on pronouns, page 4.)

N O T E : Sometimes *it's* can be short for *it has,* as in: *It's been hours since he ate.*

Who's Whose?

The battle between *whose* and *who's* comes up less frequently than the one between *its* and *it's* (see above), but the problems are identical. If you can solve one, you've got the other one whipped.

Don't be misled by the apostrophe. Not every possessive has one. *Who* (like *it* and *he*) is a pronoun—a stand-in for a noun—and pronouns don't have apostrophes when they're possessives: *"**Whose** frog is this?" said Miss Grundy.*

Now, as for *who's,* the apostrophe stands for something that has been removed. *Who's* is short for *who is,* and the apostrophe replaces the missing *i* in *is. "And **who's** responsible for putting it in my desk?"*

Here's how to keep *whose* and *who's* straight:

● If you can substitute *who is,* use *who's.* If not, use *whose.*

NOTE: Sometimes *who's* can be short for *who has,* as in: **Who's had lunch?**

Their Is But to Do or Die

His newest book, Monster Truck, *is written especially for the child with machinery on **their** mind.* Hmm . . . *their?* Let's hope this children's book is better written than the ad.

Their, the possessive form of *they,* is often used mistakenly for *his* or *her,* as in: **No one in their** right mind pays retail. Ouch! *No one* is singular, and the possessive that goes with it should be singular, too: **No one in her** right mind pays retail.

I suspect many people are reluctant to use *his* or *her* when they aren't referring to anyone in particular. But until our language has a sex-neutral possessive to use instead, we are stuck with *his,* or *her,* or the clumsy compound *his or her.* To substitute *their* may be politically correct, but it's grammatically impaired.

For problems with *their* and its sound-alikes, see the chapter on pronouns, page 14.

Group Ownership:
When Possessives
Come in Pairs

If something has two owners, who really owns it? If two people share an experience, whose experience is it? Who, in other words, gets the apostrophe when Sam and Janet spend an evening out—is it **Sam and Janet's** *evening,* or **Sam's and Janet's** *evening?*

- If two people (*Sam and Janet*) possess something (an *evening*) in common, consider them a single unit and put a single *'s* at the end: **Sam and Janet's** *evening was ruined when their date ended at the police station.*

- If two people possess something (or some things) individually, rather than jointly, each name gets an *'s*: **Sam's and Janet's** *furniture—his Danish modern, her French rococo—would never work in the same apartment.* Or **Sam's and Janet's** *couches came from the same store.*

- If the names of the two owners are replaced by pronouns (stand-ins for nouns, like *your, my, our,* etc.), don't use them side by side, as in *"***Your and my** *furniture can't live together,"* said Janet. It sounds better with the noun in between: *"***Your** *furniture and* **mine** *can't live together."*

Nobody's Fool

Body language is no problem in the possessive. Words like *anybody, everybody, somebody,* and *nobody* become possessive when you add *'s: anybody's, everybody's, somebody's, nobody's.*

When *else* is added, the *'s* goes after *else*: *"Stella is mine, and **nobody else's**," said Stanley.* This seems pretty obvious to us now, but there was a time when it was considered correct to leave the apostrophe with the pronoun: *Is that your suit of armor, Sir Lancelot, or **somebody's else**?*

For Goodness' Sake!

Some word formations are just too much for us to get our tongues around. That's the only good reason I can think of for this next exception to the usual rules on possessives.

We may do something for *pity's* sake, for *heaven's* sake, for the *nation's* sake, for our *children's* sake. But some of the "sake" phrases—for *goodness'* sake, for *conscience'* sake, for *appearance'* sake, for *righteousness'* sake—don't take the final *s* that normally follows the apostrophe. Call it tradition. I suppose our English-speaking forebears decided there was enough hissing in those words already, without adding another sibilant syllable (say those last two words five times in rapid succession).

It's often customary to drop the final *s* when forming the possessives of ancient classical names that already end in *s*: *Whose biceps were bigger, **Hercules'** or **Achilles'**?*

Are You Too Possessive?

One way to make a noun possessive is to add *'s*; another way is to put *of* in front of it.

What about using both? Are two possessives better than one? Should we say *a friend **of Jake***? Or *a friend **of Jake's***? I'll end the suspense quickly. Both are correct.

But when a pronoun is involved, make it a possessive: *a friend of **his**,* not *a friend of **him***: *Jake is a guest of my **daughter** [or **daughter's**], which makes him a guest of **mine**.*

Doing Time

Time is money, they say, and both are valuable, which may be why they're sometimes expressed in a possessive way. It's long been the custom in English that we may, if we wish, describe periods of time and amounts of money by using possessives: *After an **hour's** wait in court, Butch was given **two years'** pro-*

bation for stealing **fifty dollars'** worth of change from the collection plate.

Of course, you can say the same thing without using any possessives: *After waiting an hour in court, Butch was given two years of probation for stealing fifty dollars in change from the collection plate.*

Do You Mind Me . . . Uh . . . My Smoking?

For many of us, this one is the Gordian knot of possessive puzzles. Actually, it's not hard to untie, once you know the secret. First, let's see how you do on your own. Which of these is correct?

1. *He resents **my going**.*
2. *He resents **me going**.*

If you picked number 2, you goofed, but don't beat up on yourself. You're a member of a large and distinguished club. To see why so many of us slip up, let's look at two similar examples:

1. *He resents **my departure**.*
2. *He resents **me departure**.*

I'll bet you didn't have any trouble with that one. Obviously, number 1 is correct. *Departure* is a noun (a thing), and when it is modified or described by a pronoun (a word that stands in for a noun), the pronoun has to be a possessive: *my, his, her, your,* and so on.

Now look again at the first set of examples:

1. *He resents **my going**.*
2. *He resents **me going**.*

If you still feel like picking number 2, it's because *ing* words are chameleons. They come from verbs—*go,* in the case of *going*—and usually act like verbs. But every once in a while they step out of character and take on the role of nouns. For all intents and purposes they may as well be nouns; in this example, *going* may as well be the noun *departure.*

The $64,000 question: How do we figure out whether an *ing* word is acting like a verb or like a noun? Here's a hint: If you can substitute a noun for the *ing* word—*departure* in place of *going,* for example, or *habit* for *smoking*—then treat it like a noun. That means making the word in front a possessive (*my,* not *me*): *He can't stand **my** smoking.*

※   ※   ※

Loose Ends

The preceding explanation unties the Gordian knot, and you can stop there if you want. But there are a couple of loose ends you may want to finish off.

Sometimes it's too clumsy to use a possessive with an *ing* word—for instance, when you'd have to make a whole string of words possessive, not just one. Here's an example: *Basil objects to* **men and women kissing** *in public.* Using the possessive (*men's and women's kissing*) would create a monster. It's good to follow a rule, except when it leads you off a cliff. Since there's no way to mistake the meaning, leave it alone. But if there's just a pronoun in front, stick to the rule and make it a possessive: *Basil objects to* **our kissing** *in public.* (Not: *Basil objects to* **us kissing** *in public.*)

Another complication is the kind of sentence that can go either way:

Basil dislikes that **woman's wearing** *shorts.*

Basil dislikes that **woman wearing** *shorts.*

Both are correct, but they mean different things. In the first example, Basil dislikes shorts on the woman. In the second, he dislikes the woman herself. The lesson? Lighten up, Basil!

They Beg to Disagree

Putting Verbs in Their Place

The verb is the business end of a sentence, the sentence's reason for being. That's where the action is. Without a verb, even if it's only suggested, there's nothing going on, just a lot of nouns standing around with their hands in their pockets. A verb is easy to spot. Just look for the moving target, the center of activity, the part that tells you what's going on. No wonder the verb is often the most interesting word in a sentence.

It's also the most complicated. Because a verb expresses action, it has a dimension that other words lack—time. It has to tell you whether something happened in the past, the present, the future, or some combination of times: *sneeze, sneezed, will sneeze, would have sneezed,* and so on. The verb has another dimension, too. It varies according to the subject (who or what is performing the action): *I sneeze, he sneezes, they sneeze,* and so on.

There are plenty of reasons a verb can go astray. The most common is that it doesn't match the subject: one is singular and the other plural (*Harry and I **was sneezing***, for example). The next most common reason is that the verb's timing—its tense—is off (*Yesterday she **sneezes***).

Then there are those pesky little verbs that are as annoying as ants at a picnic, and just about as hard to tell apart: *sit* and *set, rise* and *raise, lie* and *lay.*

This makes verbs sound daunting, but they're actually not that bad. Taken one at a time (which is how you encounter them, after all), problems with verbs can be made to disappear.

Making Verbs Agreeable

Some rules of grammar may shift every eon or so, but you can bet the bank that this one will never change: Subject and verb must agree. If the subject is singular, so is the verb (*Ollie stumbles*). If the subject is plural, so is the verb (*Stan and Ollie stumble*).

If your verb (the action word) doesn't match its subject (who or what is doing the action), you probably have the wrong subject in mind. That's not unusual, since the real subject isn't always easy to see. If you find it a breeze to write a simple sentence, but start hyperventilating when a few bells and whistles are added, you're not alone. Here's what I mean:

Every part of Ollie **needs** *a massage.*

No problem. The subject (*part*) is singular, so the verb (*needs*) is singular. Now let's add a few of Ollie's aching parts:

*Every part of Ollie—his legs, his neck, his shoulders, his feet—[***needs*** *or* ***need****] a massage.*

Since the closest word is *feet,* a plural, you might be tempted to pick *need.* But in fact, the verb stays the same, *needs,* despite the added details. That's because the subject itself (*part*) hasn't changed. The key to making subject and verb agree is to correctly identify the subject, and for that you have to simplify the sentence in your mind and eliminate the extraneous stuff. Here are a couple of tips on simplifying a sentence:

- Extra information inserted between subject and verb doesn't alter the verb.

  Spring's glory **was** *lost on Ollie.*

  Spring's glory, with its birds and its flowers and its trees, **was** *lost on Ollie.*

  The subject, *glory,* is still singular, no matter how much information you add to it.

- Phrases such as *along with, as well as, in addition to,* and *together with,* inserted between subject and verb, don't alter the verb.

  Spring **was** *a tonic for Stan.*

Spring, *along with a few occasional flirtations,* **was** *a tonic for Stan.*

The subject is still *spring,* and is singular.

- Descriptions (adjectives) added to the subject don't alter the verb.

A substance **was** *stuck to Stan's shoe.*

A green, slimy, and foul-smelling substance **was** *stuck to Stan's shoe.*

The subject is *substance,* and it stays singular no matter how many disgusting adjectives you pile on.

SPLIT DECISIONS

Often the subject of a sentence—whoever or whatever is doing the action—is a two-headed creature with *or* or *nor* in the middle: **Milk or cream** *is fine, thank you.*

When both halves of the subject—the parts on either side of *or* or *nor*—are singular, so is the verb: *Neither alcohol nor tobacco* **is** *allowed.* When both halves are plural, so is the verb: *Ties or cravats* **are** *required.*

But how about when one half is singular and the other plural? Do you choose a singular or a plural verb? *Neither the eggs nor the milk [***was*** *or* ***were***] *fresh.*

The answer is simple. If the subject nearer the verb is singular, the verb is singular: *Neither the eggs nor the* **milk was** *fresh.* If the subject nearer the verb is plural, the verb is plural: *Neither the milk nor the* **eggs were** *fresh.*

The same rule applies when subjects are paired with *not only* and *but also: Not only the chairs but also the **table was** sold*. Or: *Not only the table but also the **chairs were** sold*.

THE SUBJECT WITH MULTIPLE PERSONALITIES

Say you've identified the subject of a sentence, and it's a word that could be interpreted as either singular or plural, like *couple, total, majority, number, any, all,* or *none*. Is the verb singular or plural?

Here's how to decide.

Words that stand for a group of things—*couple, total, majority,* and *number*—sometimes mean the group as a whole (singular), and sometimes mean the individual members of the group (plural). The presence of *the* before the word (*the couple, the total, the majority*) is often a clue that it's singular, so use a singular verb: *The **couple lives** in apartment 9A.* When *a* comes before the word, and especially when *of* comes after (*a couple of, a number of*), it's probably plural, so use a plural verb: *A **couple of** deadbeats **live** in apartment 9A.*

The words *all, any,* and *none* can also be either singular or plural. If you're using them to suggest *all of it, any of it,* or *none of it,* use a singular verb: ***All** the money [all of it] **is** spent.* If you're suggesting *all of them, any of them,* or *none of them,* use a plural verb: ***All** the customers [all of them] **are** gone.*

There's more about these two-edged words in the chapter on plurals, pages 25–28.

What and Whatnot

Here's another multiple personality—a word that can be either singular or plural. Take a look at these examples:

What is going on here? What are your intentions, Mister?

As you can see, *what* can be either singular or plural when it's the subject of a verb. If *what* stands for one thing, use a singular verb (*is,* in this case). If it stands for several things, use a plural verb (*are,* for example).

But how do you choose? Consider this sentence: *Phyllis is wearing **what** [look or looks] like false eyelashes.* Just ask yourself whether *what* refers to "a thing that" or "things that." In this case, she is wearing *things* that *look* like false eyelashes. Use the plural verb: *Phyllis is wearing **what look** like false eyelashes.*

> **NOTE:** When *what* affects two verbs in the same sentence, the verbs should be alike—both singular or both plural, not one of each: **What gives** *away Phyllis's* age **is** *her bad knees.* In other words, the thing about Phyllis that gives away her age is the fact that she has bad knees. On the other hand, if you want to emphasize that both of Phyllis's knees have gone bad, you should choose plurals for both verbs: **What give** *away Phyllis's age **are** her two bad knees.* As you may suspect, there can be room for disagreement about whether *what* should be singular or plural. What's important to remember is that if *what* affects two verbs, they should match—both singular or both plural.

There's more about *what* in the chapter on pronouns; see page 17.

THERE, THERE, NOW!

When a statement starts with *there*, the verb can be either singular or plural. We can say *there is* or *there are*:

*"**There is** a fly in my soup!"* said Mr. LaFong. *"And **there are** lumps in the gravy!"*

The choice can be tricky, because *there* is only a phantom subject. In the first example, the real subject is *fly*; in the second, it's *lumps*. If the subject is hard for you to see, just delete *there* in your mind and turn the statement around: *"A fly **is** in my soup! And lumps **are** in the gravy!"*

For more on *there* at the head of a sentence, see pages 184 and 192.

Wishful Thinking: I Wish I Was . . . or . . . I Wish I Were?

"Difficult do you call it, Sir?" the lexicographer Samuel Johnson once said after hearing a violinist perform. "I wish it were impossible."

Were? Why not *I wish it **was** impossible*? Well, in English we have a special way of speaking wishfully. We say, *I wish I* *were in love again,* not *I wish I was in love again.* There's a peculiar, wishful kind of grammar for talking about things that are desirable, as opposed to things as they really are. When we're in a wishful mood (a grammarian would call it the subjunctive mood), *was* becomes *were:*

I wish I were in Paris. (I'm not in Paris.)

They wish he weren't so obnoxious. (He is so obnoxious.)

She wishes New York were cleaner. (New York isn't cleaner.)

He wishes Julia were home more often. (Julia isn't home more often.)

Iffy Situations: If I Was . . . or . . . If I Were?

What a difference an *if* makes. An ordinary, straightforward statement like *I was taller* becomes quite another proposition when we insert one little word: *If I were taller.*

Why is this? It's because there's a special, "what if" sort of grammar that kicks in when we talk about something that's untrue. When we're in this iffy mood (the subjunctive mood, if you want to be technical), *was* becomes *were.* This happens when a sentence or a clause (a group of words with its own subject and verb) starts with *if,* and what's being talked about is contrary to fact:

If I were king, no one would pay retail. (I'm not king.)

*If she **were** older, she'd know better.* (She's not older.)

*We could go shopping if it **were** Saturday.* (Today is not Saturday.)

NOTE: Not all *if* statements fall into this category, only those that are undeniably contrary to fact. In cases where the statement may actually be true, *was* remains *was*.

*If I **was** rude, I apologize.* (I may have been rude.)

*If she **was** there, I guess I missed her.* (She may have been there.)

*If it **was** Thursday, I must have gone to bed early.* (It may have been Thursday.)

As If You Didn't Know

The same rules that apply to *if* statements apply to those starting with *as if* or *as though*:

*He acts as if he **were** infallible.*

(He's not infallible.)

*She behaves as though money **were** the problem.*

(Money is not the problem.)

Suggestive Language

Sometimes, English slips through a time warp and into another dimension. In cases where we'd normally use the verbs *was* or *were,* we use *be* instead. You might have wondered why we say, *I **was** quiet,* but *They requested that I **be** quiet.* What's going on here? The answer is that in English we have a special way of suggesting or demanding something (another example of the subjunctive mood). This is what you need to remember:

Use *be* instead of *was* or *were* after someone *suggests, demands, asks, requests, requires,* or *insists* that something be done:

*I demanded that I **be** excused.*

*The judge ordered that he **be** executed.*

*Olivia insists they **be** admitted free.*

*The law requires that you **be** fingerprinted.*

If *be* sounds unnatural to your ear, just imagine an unspoken *should* in front of it:

I demanded that I (should) be excused.

The judge ordered that he (should) be executed.

Olivia insisted they (should) be admitted free.

The law requires that you (should) be fingerprinted.

By the way, the form of the verb used here—*be* instead of *was* or *were*—is similar to the one used for a command: *Be good! Be quiet! Be there or **be** square!*

NOTE: Although *was, were,* and *be* give us the most trouble when we're suggesting or demanding something, other verbs must also be in the command form when they're forced to give "command" performances: *Mom demands that Ricky* **eat.** *We insist that she* **walk.** *He urged that Barbra* **negotiate.** *I suggested he go.* Again, if this feels unnatural, imagine an unspoken *should* in front of the verb: *I suggested he (should)* **go.**

Mayday! Mayday!

If there were a club for people who confuse *may* and *might,* I would be its president. Also its vice-president, treasurer, and recording secretary. I'm always using the search function on my computer to find *may* in my work, because it is often wrong and should be *might.*

May is a source of our word *maybe,* and that's a good clue to how it's used. We attach it to another verb (*happen,* for example) to indicate the possibility of something's happening. If we say something *may* happen, we mean it's possible or even probable.

Might is a slightly weaker form of *may.* Something that *might* happen is a longer shot than something that *may* happen. *I* **may** *get a raise* is more promising than *I* **might** *get a raise.*

Although your dictionary will tell you that *might* can be the past tense of *may*, either one can be used in the present tense (*She **may** break a leg; She **might** break a leg*) or in the past (*She **may** have broken a leg; She **might** have broken a leg*). The form you choose depends on the degree of possibility and can radically change your meaning. *A bulletproof vest **may** have saved him* implies that he was saved. *A bulletproof vest **might** have saved him* implies that he wasn't.

There's an exception to this rule of possibility, which is why I'm grateful for search keys. If a sentence has other verbs in the past tense, use only *might*: *She thought* [past] *she **might** have broken a leg. Eloise was* [past] *afraid they **might** lose everything. Frank said* [past] *he **might** leave early.*

Just One of Those Things

Here's one of the things that [*drives* or *drive*] us crazy. Should the verb be singular or plural? *Drives*? Or *drive*? In other words, what kind of verb goes with a phrase like *one of the, one of those,* or *one of these*? The answer in a nutshell:

- If *that* or *who* comes before the verb, it's plural: *He's one of the authors who **say** it best.*
- If not, it's singular: *One of the authors **says** it best.*

In the first example, *one* is not the subject of the verb *say*. The actual subject is *who*, which is plural because it refers to *authors.* In the second example, the subject really is *one.* If you don't trust me, just turn the sentences around in your mind and you'll end up with the correct verbs: *Of the authors who* **say** *it best, he is one. Of the authors, one* **says** *it best.*

Never-Never Land

Poor verbs! We tend to spread them a little thin sometimes. Any sentence with *never have and never will* is probably doomed. There's almost no way to finish it correctly, because so few verbs go with both *have* and *will.*

Here's the kind of sentence I mean: *They* **never have and never will** *forget Paris.* What we intend to say is, *They never have forgotten and never will forget Paris.* But what we've actually said is, *They never have [forget] and never will forget Paris.* That odd, crackling noise you hear is the sound of a sentence short-circuiting! This problem comes up when we use *have* and *will* with the same verb. Another major culprit is *always have and always will.*

Only when a verb appears the same way twice (like *forget* in *I never could forget and never would forget Paris*) can you omit the first one and avoid repeating yourself: *I never could and never would forget Paris.*

> **NOTE:** If you don't want to repeat yourself when using different forms of the same verb, you can cheat

by rearranging the sentence: *They never have forgotten Paris and never will.* That way, the part you omit—*forget Paris*—is at the end of the sentence, where it won't be missed very much. This isn't perfect grammar, mind you, but it's reasonable. And nobody will blow a fuse.

Ize in Our Heads: Are These Verbs Legit?

For centuries, we've been creating instant verbs in English simply by adding *ize* to nouns (*demon* ⇒ *demonize*, for instance) or to adjectives (*brutal* ⇒ *brutalize*). The ancient Greeks were the ones who gave us the idea. The *ize* ending (often *ise* in British spellings) has given us loads of useful words (*agonize, burglarize, fantasize, mesmerize, pasteurize, pulverize*). It's just as legitimate to add *ize* to the end of a word as it is to add *un* or *pre* to the beginning.

Yet there can be too much of a good thing, and that's what has happened with *ize*. Verbs should be lively little devils, and just adding *ize* to a word doesn't give it life. Fortunately, many recent horrors (*credibilize, permanentize, respectabilize, uniformize*) didn't catch on. But some lifeless specimens have slipped into the language, among them *colorize, prioritize,* and *finalize,* and they're probably going to be around for a while.

Infinitively Speaking

Many of us misuse the infinitive (a verb that usually has *to* in front of it) after certain words. *Anxious*, for example. Are you *anxious to go*, or are you *anxious about going*? If you picked *anxious to go*, you should be anxious about your grammar. Here's a list of words that shouldn't be followed by infinitives:

anxious: *I was* **anxious about going**. Not: *I was anxious to go*. With the infinitive, use *eager* instead: *I was* **eager to go**. For more about *anxious* and *eager*, see page 91.

convince: *They* **convinced** *us* **that** *we should go*. Not: *They convinced us to go*. With the infinitive, use *persuade*: *They* **persuaded** *us* **to** *go*. For more about *convince* and *persuade*, see page 96.

prevent: *We* **prevented** *him* **from** *going*. Not: *We prevented him to go*. If you keep the infinitive, use *did not permit* instead: *We* **did not permit** *him* **to** *go*. Another way to say this is: *We* **prevented** *his going*.

prohibit: *She was* **prohibited from** *going*. Not: *She was prohibited to go*. With the infinitive, use *forbid*: *She was* **forbidden to** *go*. For more about *forbid* and *prohibit*, see pages 111 and 113.

I have two pieces of advice about verbs ending in *ize*:

- Don't coin any new ones.
- Don't use any recent ones you don't like. If we ignore them, maybe they'll go away.

Ants at the Picnic: Pesky Look-alikes

Who hasn't confused *lie* and *lay*? *Sit, set,* and *sat*? *Rise* and *raise*? It's nothing to be ashamed of. You could commit them all to memory, of course. Or you could *lay* your cares aside, *sit* tight, *rise* to the occasion, and look up the answer.

Here's the *lay* of the land (or, as they say in Britain, the *lie* of the land):

lie (to recline): *She **lies** quietly. Last night, she **lay** quietly. For years, she **has lain** quietly.*

lie (to fib): *He **lies**. Yesterday he **lied**. Frequently he **has lied**.*

lay (to place): *She **lays** it there. Yesterday she **laid** it there. Many times she **has laid** it there.* (When *lay* means "to place," it's always followed by an object, the thing being placed.)

sit (to be seated): *I **sit**. I **sat** last week. I **have sat** many times.*

set (to place): *He **sets** it there. He **set** it there yesterday. He **has set** it there frequently.* (*Set* meaning "to place" is always followed by an object, the thing being placed.)

rise (to go up or get up): *You* **rise.** *You* **rose** *at seven. You* **have risen** *even earlier.*

raise (to bring something up): *I* **raise** *it. I* **raised** *it last year. I* **have raised** *it several times.* (The verb *raise* is always followed by an object, the thing being brought up.)

Fitted to Be Tied

Several verbs ending in *t* or *d* have all but dropped the *ed* ending in the past tense. Once we would have said, *Mr. Pecksniff* **quitted** *the firm,* **betted** *on the horses, and* **wetted** *his whistle, then* **wedded** *his sweetheart in a suit that* **fitted** *him perfectly.* The British still use those endings, but Americans are now more likely to use the shorter *quit, bet, wet, wed,* and *fit. Mr. Pecksniff* **quit** *the firm,* **bet** *on the horses, and* **wet** *his whistle, then* **wed** *his sweetheart in a suit that* **fit** *him perfectly.*

We still use *wedded,* but only as an adjective (a word that describes people or things): **Wedded** *life is a thrill a minute.*

We also use *fitted* as an adjective (*a fitted sheet, a fitted suit*). And we use *fitted* when we speak of someone whose clothes are, shall we say, under construction: *Alice was* **fitted** *for a new dress.* But later we would say, *When it was finished, the dress* **fit** *like a glove.*

Happy Endings: Burned or Burnt?

He *spilled* the milk, or he *spilt* it? He *burned* the toast, or he *burnt* it? Actually, they're all correct, although in these cases the *ed* spellings are preferred.

A number of verbs can form the past tense with either *ed* or *t*. For some of them, the preferred ending is *ed*, and for others it's *t*. In these examples, the favored spellings are given first, and the less common ones follow in parentheses: *bereaved* (*bereft*), *dreamed* (*dreamt*), *dwelt* (*dwelled*), *knelt* (*kneeled*), *leaned* (*leant*), *leaped* (*leapt*), *learned* (*learnt*), *smelled* (*smelt*), *spelled* (*spelt*), *spoiled* (*spoilt*).

> **NOTE:** Some verbs no longer have alternative *ed* endings: *bent* (the obsolete form survives in the phrase *on bended knee*), *crept*, *dealt*, *felt*, *kept*, *left*, *lost*, *meant*, *slept*, *swept*, and *wept*.

Wake-up Calls

Wake . . . woke . . . have *woken*? Or is it have *waked*? Some days it's a challenge just to get up in the morning. If you lie awake nights worrying about this one, don't bother. Either form is correct, though many dictionaries now prefer *have woken,* long favored by the British but once considered obsolete in American English.

For the record, the accepted forms of the verb *wake* are *wake, woke* (or *waked*), and *have woken* (or *have waked*). Here they are in action: *I usually* **wake** *at seven. Yesterday, I* **woke** (or **waked**) *at nine. In the past, I* **have woken** (or **have waked**) *as early as five.* By the way, it's fine to add *up* to any of the *wake* forms: *Wake* **up** *and smell the coffee!*

If you're like me, and you think both *have woken* and *have waked* sound weird, try *have wakened* or *have awakened.* Those are past tenses of related verbs, *waken* and *awaken.*

There are lots of ways to greet the morning—maybe more than we need. You can *wake,* or you can *waken,* or you can *awake,* or you can *awaken.* So rise and shine, already!

What's the Use?

One way to say *he formerly did* is *he used to: Andre* **used to** *have a good lob.*

What about when the sentence becomes a question or a negative statement? Let's see if we can choose the right form:

Did Andre [**use** or **used**] *to have a good lob?*

Andre didn't [**use** or **used**] *to have a good lob.*

The answer in both cases is *use.* Why? Because *did use* is another way of saying *used*, just as *did walk* is another way of saying *walked*. You wouldn't say "did walked," would you? Then why would you say "did used"?

> **NOTE:** The British, as you might have noticed, have a different way of dealing with *used to*. Instead of using *did* in a question or a negative statement, they prefer these forms: *Used Andre to have a good lob? Andre usedn't to have a good lob.* Forget you ever saw them.

Getting the Hang of Hung

No! It's not true that *hung* is never right. I would like to impress this on the magazine writer who described somebody's walls as "hanged with handsome black-and-white photographs."

Both past tenses have been around for hundreds of years, but since the sixteenth century it's been customary to reserve *hanged* for referring to executions, and to use *hung* for other meanings.

So, except at the gallows, *hung* is the correct past tense of *hang*: *He **hung** around. They **have hung** around.* This is true whether you've *hung* pictures, *hung* loose, *hung* out, *hung* laundry, or *hung* up.

Anyone who still uses *hanged* in such cases should be suspended.

That's That

There are two kinds of editors. One kind sticks in *that* wherever it will fit. The other kind takes it out.

They're both wrong.

Many verbs (*think, say, hope, believe, find, feel,* and *wish* are examples) sometimes sound smoother—to my ears, at least—when they're followed by *that*: *Carmela believed [**that**] Tony was unfaithful*. You may agree that the sentence sounds better with *that,* or you may not. It's purely a matter of taste. The sentence is correct either way.

Some writers and editors believe that if *that* can logically follow a verb, it should be there. Others believe that if *that* can logically be omitted, it should be taken out. If you like it, use it. If you don't, don't. Here are some cases where adding *that* can rescue a drowning sentence.

- When a time element comes after the verb: *Junior said on Friday he would pay up*. This could mean either: *Junior said **that** on Friday he would pay up,* or *Junior said on Friday **that** he would pay up*. So why not add a *that* and make yourself clear?
- When the point of the sentence comes late: *Johnny found the old violin hidden in a trunk in his attic wasn't a real Stradivarius*. Better: *Johnny found **that** the old violin hidden in a trunk in his attic wasn't a real Stradivarius*. Otherwise, we have to read to the end of the

sentence to learn that Johnny's finding the violin isn't the point.

● When there are two more verbs after the main one: *Silvio thinks the idea stinks and Paulie does too.* What exactly is Silvio thinking? The sentence could mean *Silvio thinks **that** the idea stinks and **that** Paulie does too.* Or it could mean *Silvio thinks **that** the idea stinks, and Paulie does too.* Adding *that* (and a well-placed comma) can make clear who's thinking what.

Splitsville

Many people seem to believe that there's something sacred about a verb, and that it's wrong to split up one that comes in parts (*had gone* or *would go,* for example). You've probably heard at one time or another that you're cheating if you slip a word (say, *finally*) in between (as in *had finally gone* or *would finally go*). Well, it just isn't so.

The best place to put a word like *finally*—that is, an adverb, a word that characterizes a verb—is directly before the action being described: in this case, *go* or *gone.* It's perfectly natural to split the parts of a verb like *have gone* by putting an adverb between them: *The goombahs **have finally gone**.* If you prefer to put the adverb before or after all the parts of the verb (as in, *The goombahs **finally have gone**,* or *The goombahs **have gone finally**,*), that's all right, too. But don't go out of your way to avoid the "splits." And keep in mind that adverbs usually do the most good right in front of the action words they describe.

This fear of splitting verb phrases, by the way, has its origins in another old taboo—the dreaded "split infinitive" (*to finally go,* for instance). The chapter on dead rules has more on that one, and on how the myth got started. See pages 182 and 185.

The Willies: Will or Shall?

In George Washington's day, schoolchildren on both sides of the Atlantic were admonished to use *shall* instead of *will* in some cases. (Don't ask!) Americans have since left *shall* behind and now use *will* almost exclusively. Although *shall* survives in parts of England, even the British are using it less and less these days.

Shall can still be found in a few nooks and crannies of American English, such as legalese (*This lease* **shall** *commence on January 1*) and lofty language (*We* **shall** *overcome*). It's also used with *I* and *we* in some kinds of questions—when we're asking what another person wishes: **Shall** *we dance, or* **shall** *I fill your glass?*

Shall is one of the "living dead" discussed in the chapter on outdated rules, page 189.

The Incredible Shrinking Words: Contractions

The contraction—two words combined into one, as in *don't* or *I'm*—seldom gets a fair shake from English teachers. It may be tolerated, but it's looked down upon as colloquial or, according to one expert, "dialect" (what a slur!). Yet despite its esteem problem, the humble contraction is used every day by virtually everyone, and has been for centuries. Quaint antiquities like *shan't* (shall not), *'tis* (it is), *'twas* (it was), *'twill* (it will), *'twould* (it would), and even *'twon't* (it will not) are evidence of the contraction's long history.

Today's contractions usually include a verb, along with a subject or the word "not."

Isn't it time we admitted that the contraction has earned its place in the sun? It has all the qualities we admire in language: it's handy, succinct, and economical, and everybody knows what it means. Contractions are obviously here to stay, so why not give them a little respect? Here's the long and the short of it: the contractions that are respectable, followed by a few that aren't.

FIT TO PRINT

aren't	are not	mustn't	must not
can't	cannot	oughtn't	ought not
couldn't	could not	she'd	she would;
didn't	did not		she had
doesn't	does not	she'll	she will
don't	do not	she's	she is;
hadn't	had not		she has
hasn't	has not	shouldn't	should not
haven't	have not	that's	that is;
he'd	he would;		that has
	he had	there's	there is;
he'll	he will		there has
he's	he is;	they'd	they would;
	he has		they had
I'd	I would;	they'll	they will
	I had	they're	they are
I'll	I will	they've	they have
I'm	I am	wasn't	was not
I've	I have	we'd	we would;
isn't	is not		we had
it'll	it will	we'll	we will
it's	it is; it has	we're	we are
let's	let us	we've	we have
mightn't	might not	weren't	were not

what'll	what will	who's	who is;
what're	what are		who has
what's	what is;	who've	who have
	what has	won't	will not
what've	what have	wouldn't	would not
where's	where is	you'd	you would;
who'd	who would;		you had
	who had	you'll	you will
who'll	who will	you're	you are
who're	who are	you've	you have

Out of Bounds

ain't. It's not OK and it never will be OK. Get used to it. If you're tempted to use it to show that you have the common touch, make clear that you know better: *Now, **ain't** that a shame!*

could've, should've, would've, might've, must've. There's a good reason to stay away from writing these. Seen in print, they encourage mispronunciation, which explains why they're often heard as *could of, should of, would of, might of,* and *must of* (or, even worse, *coulda, shoulda, woulda, mighta,* and *musta*). It's fine to pronounce these as though the *h* in *have* were silent. But let's not forget that *have* is there. Write it out.

gonna, gotta, wanna. These are merely substandard English. Unless you're talking to your sister on the phone, make it *going to, got to, want to,* and so on.

how'd, how'll, how're, how's, when'll, when're, when's, where'd, where'll, where're, why'd, why're, why's. Resist the urge to write any contractions with *how, when, where,* or *why,* except that old standby *where's.* We all say things like, *"How'm I supposed to pay for this?"* But don't put them in writing.

it'd, that'd, there'd, this'd, what'd. Notice how these *'d* endings seem to add a syllable that lands with a *thud?* And they look ridiculously clumsy in writing. Let's use the *'d* contractions (for *had* or *would*) only with *I, you, he, she, we, they,* and *who.*

that'll, that're, that've, there'll, there're, there've, this'll. Ugh! These clumsies may be fine in conversation, but written English isn't ready for them yet. Do I use *that'll* when I talk? Sure. But not when I write.

Where There's a Will, There's a Would

Do you waffle when faced with the choice of *will* or *would*? Take your pick: *Harry said he [**will** or **would**] make waffles for breakfast.*

All Tensed Up

If we used only one verb per sentence, we'd never have trouble choosing the tense—past, present, future, or whatever: *They waltzed. He tangos. She will polka.* And so on. Many sentences, though, have several things going on in them—actions happening at different times, each with its own verb. You can't just string these verbs together like beads in a necklace. It takes planning.

With most sentences, we don't give this much thought, and we don't have to. When all the actions happen at about the same time, we can just put them in the same tense and rattle them off in order: *On Sundays, Elaine **rises** at seven, **makes** tea, **showers**, and **goes** back to bed. Last Sunday, Elaine **rose** at seven, **made** tea, **showered**, and **went** back to bed.*

When we have different things happening at distinctly different times, sentences get more complicated: *Elaine **says** she **made** tea last Sunday, but she **will make** coffee next week.*

Common sense tells us how to do most of these adjustments in timing. But some verb sequences are harder to sort out than others. Pages 77–80 deal with some of the most troublesome ones.

Follow the lead of the first verb (*said*). Since it's in the past tense, use *would*: *Harry said he **would** make waffles for breakfast*. When the first verb is in the present tense (*says*), use *will*: *Harry says he **will** make waffles for breakfast*.

Now here's an example with three verbs (the same principle applies): *Harry thought that if he [**eats** or **ate**] one waffle, he [**will** or **would**] want another*.

Since the first verb (*thought*) is in the past, use the past tense, *ate*, and *would*: *Harry thought that if he **ate** one waffle, he **would** want another*. When the first verb is in the present (*thinks*), use the present tense, *eats*, and *will*: *Harry thinks that if he **eats** one waffle, he **will** want another*.

In the Land of If

Think of *if* as a tiny set of scales. When a sentence has *if* in it, the verbs have to be in balance. When the *if* side of the scale is in the present tense, the other side calls for *will*. When the *if* side of the scale is in the past tense, the other side gets a *would*.

*If he **shops** [present] alone, he **will spend** too much.*

*If he **shopped** [past] alone, he **would spend** too much.*

Balancing the scales becomes more complicated as the tenses get more complicated. When you use a compound tense with *has* or *have* on the *if* side of the scale, you need a *will have* on the other side. Similarly, when you use a compound tense with *had* on the *if* side of the scale, you need a *would have* on the other.

*If he **has shopped** alone, he **will have spent** too much.*

*If he **had shopped** alone, he **would have spent** too much.*

The *if* part doesn't have to come first, but the scales must stay in balance: *He **will spend** too much if he **shops** alone. He **would spend** too much if he **shopped** alone.*

After Thoughts

Some people tense up when one action comes after another in a sentence. Let's test your tension level. Which verbs would be better in these examples?

*I will start dinner after the guests [**arrive** or **have arrived**].*

*I started dinner after the guests [**arrived** or **had arrived**].*

If you chose the simpler ones, you were right: *I will start dinner after the guests **arrive**. I started dinner after the guests **arrived**.* Why make things harder than they have to be?

No matter what the tense of the main part of a sentence, and no matter how complicated, the verb that follows *after* should be in either the simple present (*arrive*) or the simple past (*arrived*).

When the main action in a sentence takes place in the present or in a future tense, the verb that follows *after* is in the simple present:

*I start dinner after the guests **arrive**. I will have started dinner after the guests **arrive**.*

When the main action takes place in a past tense, the verb that follows *after* is in the simple past:

*I would have started dinner after the guests **arrived**.*

The rule is the same if the sentence is turned around so the *after* part comes first: *After the guests **arrive**, I will have started dinner.*

Sometimes the simple solution is the best. Keep that in mind, and may all your verbs live happily ever after.

To Have or Not to Have

Have is a useful word, but we can have too much of it.

Which is correct? *I would have liked **to go**,* or *I would have liked **to have gone**.*

The first example is correct. One *have* is enough, though it can go with whichever half of the sentence you want to emphasize: *I would **have** liked to go,* or *I would like to **have** gone.*

Here's a case in which even one *have* is a *have* too many.

Incorrect: *Two years ago, Whiskers was the first cat to have flown on the Concorde.*

Correct: *Two years ago, Whiskers was the first cat to fly on the Concorde.*

You need to use *have* only if you're talking about two different times in the past: *Until last year, Whiskers was the only cat **to have flown** on the Concorde.* If you find the concept hard to grasp, think of it this way. One of the times was last year and the other was the period before that.

I could go on about the subtleties of *have,* but I suspect that by now you've had it.

Chapter 5

Verbal Abuse

Words on the Endangered List

The give-and-take of language is something like warfare. A word bravely soldiers on for years, until one day it falls face-down in the trenches, its original meaning a casualty of mis-use. *Unique* is a good example: a crisp and accurate word meaning "one of a kind," now frequently degraded to merely "unusual."

Then there are what I call mixed doubles: pairs of words and phrases that are routinely confused, like *affect* and *effect*. Finally, there are the words that are mispronounced, mis-spelled, or so stretched out of shape that they aren't even words anymore—like that impostor *irregardless*.

Keep in mind, though, that today's clumsy grotesquerie may be tomorrow's bon mot. Dictionaries are forever chang-ing their minds about what's acceptable, and they're sup-posed to. Their job is to reflect the language people use at a particular time—the good, the bad, the indifferent. So spellings, pronunciations, and meanings that once were considered substandard or even illiterate (words like *irregardless,* spellings like *alright,* pronunciations like NOO-kyoo-lur) may find acceptance in dictionaries as more people use them. But what's common isn't necessarily correct.

If correctness is what you're after, your computer spell-checker may only add to the confusion. Mine tells me, for instance, that *restauranteur* and *judgement* and *straightlaced* are preferred spellings, but I know better. And it doesn't care whether I use *affect* or *effect.* There's more about spell-checkers in the chapter on e-mail, page 214.

What's a reasonable person to do? Let's take a closer look at some of the more commonly mauled words and phrases. Where authorities disagree, I've tried to weigh the best evidence and make decisions that reflect what thoughtful, literate people consider good English.

Here, then, are the walking wounded. Bloodied but unbowed, they shouldn't be given up for dead. Give them back their proper meaning, spelling, usage, and pronunciation, and they'll live to fight another day.

What's the Meaning of This?

decimate. Who says grammar books don't have sex and violence? To *decimate* means literally "to slaughter every tenth one," although most people don't intend it literally. It can be used loosely to mean "to destroy in part" (*Gomez says the mushroom crop in the cellar has been decimated by rats*), but don't use it to mean "to destroy entirely." And definitely don't attach a figure to the damage: *The earthquake decimated seventy-five percent of Morticia's antiques.* Ouch!

diagnose. The disease is *diagnosed,* not the patient. *Miss Mapp's rash was diagnosed as shingles.* Not: *Miss Mapp was diagnosed with shingles.*

dilemma. This is no ordinary problem; the *di* (from the Greek for "twice") is a clue that there's a *two*ness here. A *dilemma* is a situation involving at least two choices—all of them bad. (This idea is captured neatly in the old phrase about being caught on the *horns of a dilemma.*) *Richie faced a dilemma: he could wear the green checked suit with the gravy stain, or the blue one with the hole.*

eclectic. This word is mistakenly used to mean discriminating or sophisticated; in fact, it means "drawn from many sources." *Sherman has an eclectic assortment of mud-wrestling memorabilia.*

effete. Don't use this if you mean weak, effeminate, soft, or affected. *Effete* means barren, used up, or worn out. *Frazier considers abstract expressionism an effete art form.*

enervating. Energizing it's not. On the contrary: if something's *enervating,* it drains you of energy. *Frazier's date found his conversation enervating.*

enormity. Don't confuse this with *enormousness,* because *enormity* isn't a measure of size alone. It refers to something immensely wicked, monstrous, or outrageous. *Sleepy little Liechtenstein was shocked by the **enormity** of the crime.*

fortuitous. No, this word doesn't mean fortunate. Formally speaking, *fortuitous* means accidental. (*It was entirely **fortuitous** that Ralph bought a filly instead of a colt.*) Still, those notions of good fortune and chance have blended so much that dictionaries now accept a hybrid definition—something *fortuitous* is a happy accident. (*Pie-O-My was a **fortuitous** choice.*) The upshot? To avoid misunderstanding, use another word to describe an *un*lucky accident.

fulsome. You may think this means abundant; it also means overdone or disgustingly excessive. *Eddie's insincere and **fulsome** speeches got on Mrs. Cleaver's nerves.* Avoid it if you might be misunderstood.

hero. There was a time when this word was reserved for people who were . . . well . . . heroic. People who performed great acts of bravery or valor, often facing danger, even death. But lately, *hero* has started losing its luster. We hear it applied indiscriminately to professional athletes, lottery winners, and kids who clean up at spelling bees. There's no other word quite like *hero,* so let's not bestow it too freely. It would be a pity to lose it. *Achilles was a **hero**.*

hopefully. These days, it's hopeless to resist the evolution of *hopefully*. Purists used to insist (and some still do) that there's only one way to use it correctly—as an adverb meaning "in a hopeful manner." (*"I'm thinking of going to Spain," Eddie told Mrs. Cleaver. "Soon?" she asked **hopefully**.*) If the holdouts had their way, nobody would use *hopefully* to replace a phrase like "it is hoped" or "let us hope," as in: *"**Hopefully** the cuisine in Spain will be as delectable as your own," Eddie said.* But here in the real world, language changes, and upright citizens have been using *hopefully* in that looser way for ages. It's time to admit that *hopefully* has joined that class of introductory words (like *fortunately, frankly, happily, honestly, sadly, seriously,* and others) that we use not to describe a verb, which is what adverbs usually do, but to describe our attitude toward the statement that follows. The technical term for them is sentence adverbs. When I say, "Sadly, Eddie stayed for dinner," I probably don't mean that Eddie was sad about staying. I mean, "I'm sad to say that Eddie stayed for dinner." And "Frankly, he's boring" doesn't mean the poor guy is boring in a frank way. It means, "I'm being frank when I say he's boring." Frankly, I see no reason to treat *hopefully* otherwise. But be aware that some sticklers still take a narrow view of *hopefully*. Will they ever join the crowd? One can only hope.

irony. I hope some TV news reporters are tuning in. A wonderful word for a wonderful idea, *irony* refers to a sly form of expression in which you say one thing and mean another. (*"You're wearing the green checked suit again, Richie! How fashionable of you," said Mrs. Cunningham, her voice full of **irony**.*) A situation is *ironic* when the result is the opposite—or pretty much so—of what was intended. It isn't merely coincidental or surprising, as when the newscaster thoughtlessly reports, "Ironically, the jewelry store was burglarized on the same date last year." If the burglars take great pains to steal what turns out to contain a homing device that leads the police to them, that's *ironic*. (And forget the correct but clunky *ironical*.)

literally. This means actually or to the letter. (*Martha sprayed a dried bouquet with metallic paint, **literally** gilding the lily*.) *Literally* is often confused with *figuratively*, which means metaphorically or imaginatively. No one says *figuratively*, of course, because it doesn't have enough oomph. I am reminded of a news story, early in my editing career in Iowa, about a Pioneer Days celebration, complete with covered wagons and costumed "settlers." Our reporter proposed to say that spectators "were literally turned inside out and shot backwards in time." Gee, we should have sent a photographer along. (For the proper use of *backward*, see **toward**, page 117.)

long-lived. How do you pronounce the *i*—like the one in "life," or the one in "to live"? Both ways are acceptable, but the first is preferred. In fact, *-lived* (as in *short-lived*, *clean-lived*, *nine-lived*, and so on) comes from the word *life* and started out as *-lifed*. That's why those in the know make these *i*'s rhyme: *"Here's to life!" cried the **long-lived** Carmine*.

noisome. If you think this means noisy, you're not even close. *Noisome* and *noisy* are as different as your nose and your ear. *Noisome* means evil-smelling or offensive. It's related to *annoy*, so think of it as a clipped form of *annoysome. The **noisome** fumes of the stink bomb forced officials to evacuate the school.*

nonplussed. It means baffled or confused, not calm and collected. *Tony was **nonplussed** at finding his golf clubs in the driveway.* (Hint: *Non* means "no," and *plus* means "more." A guy who's *nonplussed* is so perplexed he can do no more.)

presently. Misuse strikes again. If Kramer tells his landlord he's *presently* sending his rent, does that mean . . . uh . . . the check is in the mail, or the check really *is* in the mail? The answer is, don't hold your breath. *Presently* doesn't mean now or at present. It means soon, before long, any minute (hour, day) now, forthwith, shortly, keep your shirt on, faster than you can say Jack Robinson, or when I'm darn good and ready.

restive. Here's one that's worse than it sounds. *Restive* doesn't mean impatient or fidgety (that's *restless*). It means unruly or stubborn. *Even on a good day, Pugsley is a **restive** child.*

scarify. Sounds terrifying, doesn't it? Well, it's not. *Scarify* doesn't mean scare. Primarily, it means cut or scratch marks into the surface of something. A memory hint: If you *scarify* something, you leave *scars*. *Ricky promised that his Rollerblades wouldn't **scarify** the floor.*

unique. If it's *unique*, it's the one and only. It's unparalleled, without equal, incomparable, nonpareil, unrivaled, one of a kind. There's nothing like it—anywhere. There are no degrees of uniqueness, because the unique is absolute. Nothing can be more, less, sort of, rather, quite, very, slightly, or particularly *unique*. The word stands alone, like *dead, unanimous,* and *pregnant. The Great Wall of China is* **unique**.

via. This means "by way of," not "by means of." *Itzhak drove to Tanglewood* **via** *Boston.* Not: *Itzhak drove to Tanglewood* **via** *car.*

Mixed Doubles

abjure/adjure. The first means swear off. The second means command. *"***Abjure** *cigars or move out of the house!" Ethel* **adjured** *Fred.*

abridge/bridge. To *abridge* something is to shorten it (think of the word *abbreviate*). An *abridged* book, for instance, is a condensed version. To *bridge* something means what you'd expect—to connect or to span a gap. *The producers hope to* **abridge** *Philip's nine-hour opera about an engineer who tries to* **bridge** *the Grand Canyon.*

accept/except. To *accept* something is to take it or agree to it. *Except* can also be a verb—it means exclude or leave out—but its usual meaning is "other than." *"I never* **accept** *presents from men," said Lorelei, "***except** *when we've been properly introduced."*

adverse/averse. The longer word is the stronger word. *Adverse* implies hostility or opposition, and usually characterizes a thing or an action. *Averse* implies reluctance or unwillingness, and usually characterizes a person. *Georgie was not **averse** to inoculation, until he had an **adverse** reaction to the vaccine.*

affect/effect. If you're referring to a thing (a noun), ninety-nine times out of a hundred you mean *effect*. (*The termites had a startling **effect** on the piano.*) If you mean an action (a verb), the odds are just as good if you go for *affect*. (*The problem **affected** Lucia's recital.*)

> **NOTE:** Then there's that one time out of a hundred. Here are the less common meanings for each of these words:
>
> ● *Affect,* when used as a noun (pronounced with the accent on the first syllable), is a psychological term for "feeling." *Termites display a lack of **affect**.*
> ● *Effect,* when used as a verb, means achieve or bring about. *An exterminator **effected** the removal of the termites.*

aggravate/irritate. Don't use them interchangeably. Use *irritate* to mean inflame, *aggravate* to mean worsen. *Poison ivy **irritates** the skin. Scratching **aggravates** the itch.*

Aggravate is widely used to mean vex or annoy, but sticklers find this irritating.

ago/since. Use one or the other, not both. *Fluffy died three days **ago**.* Or: *It's been three days **since** Fluffy died.* Not: *It's been three days **ago since** Fluffy died.*

allude/refer. To *allude* is to mention indirectly or to hint at—to speak of something in a covert or roundabout way. (*Cyril suspected that the discussion of bad taste **alluded** to his loud pants.*) To *refer* is to mention directly. (*"They're plaid!" said Gussie, **referring** to Cyril's trousers.*)

allusion/illusion/delusion. An *allusion* is an indirect mention. (*Gussie's comment about burlesque was a snide **allusion** to Cyril's hand-painted tie.*) An *illusion* is a false impression. (*It created the **illusion** of a naked woman.*) A *delusion* is a deception. (*Cyril clung to the **delusion** that his tie was witty.*) *Delusion* is much stronger than *illusion,* and implies that Cyril has been misled or deceived—in this case, by himself.

alternate/alternative. The first means one after the other; the second means one instead of the other. *Walking requires **alternate** use of the left foot and the right. The **alternative** is to take a taxi.*

among/between. When only two are involved, the answer is easy: *between*. (*Miss Bennet sensed a barrier **between** her and Mr. Darcy.*) With three or more, you have a choice. Use *between* if you're thinking of the individuals and their relations with one another. (*There were several embarrassing exchanges **between** Lydia, Kitty, and Jane.*) Use *among* if you're thinking of the group. (*Darcy's arrival created a stir **among** the guests.*)

amused/bemused. If you're having a good time, you're *amused*. If you're befuddled or puzzled or plunged deep in thought, you're *bemused*. *"I fail to see why you're **amused**,"* *said the **bemused** Mr. Peepers, whose missing spectacles were perched on his head.*

anxious/eager. In ordinary speech, these are used interchangeably. But in writing, use *eager* unless there is actually an element of *anxiety* involved. And note that *eager* is followed by *to*, but *anxious* is followed by *about* or *for*. *Nancy is **eager** to have a pony, but Aunt Fritzi is **anxious** about the expense.* For more on these, see page 63.

appraise/apprise. *Appraise* means evaluate or size up; *apprise* means inform. *Sotheby's **apprised** Mr. Big of the fact that his "Rembrandt" was **appraised** as worthless.*

as if/as though. These mean the same thing and can be used interchangeably. Once upon a time, *if* was one of the meanings of *though*. It's not anymore, except in the phrase *as though*. *Cliff and Norm looked **as though** they could use a drink.*

assume/presume. They're not identical. *Assume* is closer to suppose, or "take for granted"; the much stronger *presume* is closer to believe, dare, or "take too much for granted." *I can only **assume** you are joking when you **presume** to call yourself a plumber!*

> **NOTE:** *Presume* in the sense of believe gives us the adjective *presumptive*. And *presume* in the sense of "take too much for granted" gives us the adjective *pre-*

*sumptuous. As her favorite nephew, Bertie was Aunt Agatha's **presumptive** heir. Still, it was **presumptuous** of him to measure her windows for new curtains.*

assure/ensure/insure. All three have their roots in a Latin word for "safe" or "secure." In American English, to *assure* is to instill confidence or certainty. As for *ensure* and *insure,* both can mean to make certain of something, but only *insure* is used in the commercial sense (to issue or take out insurance). *"I **assure** you," said the grieving widow, "I **ensured** he was **insured** to the hilt."*

avert/avoid. *Avert* means prevent, ward off, or turn away. *Avoid* means shun or stay clear of. *Mr. Smithers **avoided** the open manhole, **averting** a nasty fall.*

bad/badly. When it's an activity being described, use *badly,* the adverb (a word that describes a verb; many adverbs, you'll notice, end in *ly*). When it's a condition or a passive state being described, use *bad,* the adjective (a word that describes a noun). *Josh ran the race **badly**; afterward, he looked **bad** and he smelled **bad**.* If the difference still eludes you, try mentally substituting a pair of words less likely to be confused: *Josh ran the race **honestly**; afterward, he looked **honest** and he smelled **honest**.*

The same logic applies for *well* and *good.* When it's an activity being described, use *well,* the adverb. (As you can see, not all adverbs end in *ly.*) When it's a condition or a passive state being described, use *good,* the adjective.

Donna sang **well**; *at the recital she looked* **good** *and she sounded* **good**.

NOTE: There's a complication with *well*. It's a two-faced word that can be an adjective as well as an adverb. As an adjective, it means healthy (*Josh feels* **well**).

beside/besides. *Beside* means "by the side of." *Besides* means "in addition" or "moreover." *Pip was seated* **beside** *Miss Havisham in an uncomfortable chair. He had a fly in his soup* **besides**.

bi/semi. In theory, *bi* attached to the front of a word means two and *semi* means half. (*Although Moose is* **bi***lingual, he's* **semi***literate.*) In practice, *bi* sometimes means *semi*, and *semi* sometimes means *bi*. You're better off avoiding them when you want to indicate time periods; instead, use "every two years" or "twice a week" or whatever. I don't recommend using the following terms, but in case you run across them, here's what they mean. (You can see why they're confusing.)

biennial: every two years
biannual: twice a year *or* every two years (Here again, dictionaries tend to disagree, so they aren't much help.)
semiannual: every half-year
bimonthly: every two months *or* twice a month
semimonthly: every half-month
biweekly: every two weeks *or* twice a week
semiweekly: every half-week

both/as well as. Use one or the other, but not both. *Carrie had **both** a facial and a massage.* Or: *Carrie had a facial **as well as** a massage.*

bring/take. Which way is the merchandise moving? Is it coming or going? If it's coming here, someone's *bringing* it. If it's going there, someone's *taking* it. (***Bring** me my slippers," said Samantha, "and **take** away these stiletto heels!"*) That much is pretty straightforward, but there are gray areas where the *bringing* and the *taking* aren't so clear. Say you're a dinner guest and you decide to tote a bottle of wine along with you. Do you *bring* it or do you *take* it? The answer depends on your perspective—on which end of the journey you're talking about, the origin or the destination. "What shall I bring, white or red?" you ask the host. "Bring red," he replies. (Both you and he are speaking of the wine from the point of view of its destination—the host.) Ten minutes later, you're asking the wine merchant, "What should I take, a Burgundy or a Bordeaux?" "Take this one," she says. (Both you and she are speaking of the wine from the point of view of its origin.) Clear? If not, pour yourself a glass, take it easy, and say what sounds most natural. You'll probably be right.

callous/callus. One's an adjective (it characterizes something), and one's a noun. *Hard-hearted Hannah is **callous**, but the thing on her toe is a **callus**.*

can/may. The difference is between being able and being allowed or permitted. *Can* means able to; *may* means permitted to. *"I **can** fly when lift plus thrust is greater* *than load plus drag," said Sister Bertrille. "May I demon-strate?"*

NOTE: *May* is used in another sense: to indicate possibility. See the section on *may* and *might*, page 105.

chord/cord. A *chord* is a combination of musical notes; it has an *h*, for "harmony," which is what *chords* can produce. (*"That* **chord** *is a diminished seventh," said Ludwig.*) A *cord* is a string or cable, like the ones found in the human anatomy: spinal cord, umbilical cord, and vocal cords. (*Wolfgang never had to worry about tripping over an electrical* **cord.**) A mislaid rope may be called a *lost cord,* but the familiar musical phrase is *lost chord.*

compare with/compare to. Don't lose sleep over this one. The difference is subtle. *Compare with,* the more common phrase, means "to examine for similarities and differences." The less common *compare to* is used to show a resemblance: **Compared with** *Oscar, Felix is a crybaby. He once* **compared** *his trials* **to** *those of Job.*

complement/compliment. To *complement* is to complete, to round out, or to bring to perfection; a *complement* is something that completes or makes whole. (A little memory aid: Both *complement* and *complete* contain two *e*'s.) To *compliment* is to praise or admire; a *compliment* is an expression of praise or admiration. *Marcel loved to* **compliment** *Albertine. "That chemise* **complements** *your eyes, my little sparrow," he murmured.*

continually/continuously. Yes, there is a slight difference, although most people (and even many dictionaries) treat them the same. *Continually* means repeatedly, with breaks in between. *Continuously* means without interruption, in an unbroken stream. *Heidi has to wind the cuckoo clock **continually** to keep it running **continuously**.* (If it's important to emphasize the distinction, it's probably better to use *periodically* or *intermittently* instead of *continually* to describe something that starts and stops.) The same distinction, by the way, applies to *continual* and *continuous,* the adjective forms.

convince/persuade. You *convince* her *of* something. You *persuade* her *to do* something. *Convince* is usually followed by *of* or *that,* and *persuade* is followed by *to. Father **convinced** Bud **that** work would do him good, and **persuaded** him **to** get a job.* For more about *convince* and *persuade,* see page 63.

credibility/credulity. If you've got *credibility,* you're believable; you can be trusted. *Credulity* is a different quality—it means you'll believe whatever you're told; you're too trusting. The descriptive terms (adjectives) are *credible* (believable) and *credulous* (gullible). The opposites of these, respectively, are *incredible* (unbelievable) and *incredulous* (skeptical). *Councilman Windbag has lost his **credibility**, even among suckers known for their **credulity**.*

NOTE: Out in left field, meanwhile, is an entirely different player: *creditable,* which means deserving of credit, or praiseworthy.

deserts/desserts. People who get what they *deserve* are getting their *deserts*—the accent for both is on the second syllable. (*John Wilkes Booth got his just* **deserts**.) People who get goodies smothered in whipped cream and chocolate sauce at the end of a meal are getting *desserts*—which they may or may not deserve: *"For* **dessert** *I'll have one of those layered puff-pastry things with cream filling and icing on top," said Napoleon.* (As for the arid wasteland, use one *s* and stress the first syllable: *In the* **desert**, *August is the cruelest month.*)

differ from/differ with. In general, things *differ from* one another, but people who disagree *differ with* one another. (*Seymour insisted that his left foot* **differed from** *his right in size. His chiropodist, however,* **differed with** *him.*) In either sense, *differ* may be used alone: *Seymour says his feet differ. His chiropodist differs.*

different from/different than. What's the difference? The simple answer is that *different from* is almost always right, and *different than* is almost always wrong. You can stop there if you like.

> **NOTE:** You may use either one just before a clause (a group of words with its own subject and verb). Both of these are accepted: *Respectability is* **different from** *what it was fifty years ago. Respectability is* **different than** *it was fifty years ago.*

discomfit/discomfort. Here's a horse that's gotten out of the barn. Back when men were men and words had some muscle, *discomfit* meant defeat, rout, or overthrow. A *discomfited* enemy may well have been a dead enemy. (*Robin Hood and his merry men* **discomfited** *the Sheriff of Nottingham.*) But *discomfit* has lost its punch. Perhaps because of confusion with *discomfort* and *dismay,* it is widely used to indicate uneasiness or vague dissatisfaction. Dictionaries now accept this usage, a development I find *discomforting.*

discreet/discrete. If you're gossiping, you probably want *discreet,* a word that means careful or prudent. The other spelling, *discrete,* means separate, distinct, or unconnected. *Arthur was* **discreet** *about his bigamy. He managed to maintain two* **discrete** *households.*

disinterested/uninterested. They're not the same. *Disinterested* means impartial or neutral; *uninterested* means bored or lacking interest. *A good umpire should be* **disinterested,** *said Casey, but certainly not* **uninterested.**

each other/one another. The rule: Use *each other* for two, *one another* for three or more. (*Nick and Nora found* **each other** *adorable. Nick and his cousins all heartily despised* **one another.**) You'll never go wrong by following the rule, but keep in mind that many respected writers ignore it, using *one another* when referring to a pair. (*Husband and wife should respect* **one another.**) So if the more relaxed usage sounds better to your ear and you're not concerned about being strictly correct, allow yourself some latitude. (Speaking of *other* and *another,* here's a whole other issue. Some people jumble *whole other* with *another* and end up with *a whole nother*. Ugh! Not that you or I would ever do such a thing, of course.)

e.g./i.e. Go ahead. Be pretentious in your writing and toss in an occasional *e.g.* or *i.e.* But don't mix them up. Clumsy inaccuracy can spoil that air of authority you're shooting for. *E.g.* is short for a Latin term, *exempli gratia,* that means "for example." (*Kirk and Spock had much in common,* **e.g.,** *their interest in astronomy and their concern for the ship and its crew.*) The more specific term *i.e.,* short for the Latin *id est,* means "that is." (*But they had one obvious difference,* **i.e.,** *their ears.*) Both *e.g.* and *i.e.* must have commas before and after (unless, of course, they're preceded by a dash or a parenthesis).

emigrate/immigrate. You *emigrate from* one country and *immigrate to* another. (*Grandma* **emigrated from** *Hungary in 1923, the same year that Grandpa* **immigrated to** *America.*) Whether you're called an *emigrant* or an *immigrant* depends on whether you're going or coming, and on the point of view of the speaker. A trick for remembering:

> *E*migrant as in *Exit.*
> *I*mmigrant as in *In.*

eminent/imminent/immanent. If you mean famous or superior, the word you want is *eminent*. If you mean impending or about to happen, the word is *imminent*. If you mean inherent, present, or dwelling within, the word is the rarely heard *immanent*. *The **eminent** Archbishop Latour, knowing his death was **imminent**, felt God was **immanent**.*

> **NOTE:** The legal term is *eminent domain*.

farther/further. Use *farther* when referring to physical distance; use *further* to refer to abstract ideas or to indicate a greater extent or degree. *Lumpy insisted that he could walk no **farther**, and he refused to discuss it any **further**.*

faze/phase. To *faze* is to disconcert or embarrass; it comes from a Middle English word, *fesen*, which meant "drive away" or "put to flight." A *phase*, from the Greek word for "appear," is a stage or period of development; the word is used as a verb in the expressions *phase in* and *phase out*, to appear and disappear by stages. *Jean-Paul's infidelity is just a **phase**, says Simone, so she never lets it **faze** her.*

fewer/less. Use *fewer* to mean a smaller number of individual things; use *less* to mean a smaller quantity of something. *Mr. Flanders is a practical man. The **less** money he makes, the **fewer** dollars he spends.*

flounder/founder. To *flounder* is to stumble awkwardly or thrash about like a fish out of water. (*Harry **flounders** from one crisis to another.*) To *founder* is to collapse, fail completely, or sink like a ship. (*His business **foundered** when the market collapsed.*)

flout/flaunt. *Flout* means defy or ignore. *Flaunt* means show off. *When Bruce ran that stop sign, he was **flouting** the law and **flaunting** his new Harley.*

gantlet/gauntlet. You run the *gantlet,* but you throw down the *gauntlet.* Why? It seems that in days of yore, a knight in a fighting mood would defiantly fling his *gauntlet* (a heavy, armored glove) to the ground as a challenge. To pick up the *gauntlet* was to accept the challenge. Meanwhile, a form of military punishment (a *gantlet,* from the Swedish word for the ordeal) required the hapless offender to run between parallel lines of his colleagues, who hit him with switches or clubs as he passed. *Wearing her mink to the ASPCA meeting, Tiffany ran a **gantlet** of hostile stares. "So what?" she said, throwing down the **gauntlet**.* It's a distinction worth preserving, even if some dictionaries no longer think so.

good/well. These are cousins to **bad/badly** (page 92).

historic/historical. If something has a place in history, it's *historic.* If something has to do with the subject of history, it's *historical. There's not much **historical** evidence that the Hartletops' house is **historic**.*

hyper/hypo. Added to the front of a word, *hyper* means over or more; *hypo* means under or less. *I become **hyper**active and get a rash if I don't use a **hypo**allergenic soap.*

if/whether. When you're talking about a choice between alternatives, use *whether: Richie didn't know **whether** he should wear the blue suit or the green one.* The giveaway is the presence of *or* between the alternatives. But if there's a *whether or not* choice (*Richie wondered **whether or not** he should wear his green checked suit*), you can usually drop the *or not* and use either *whether* or *if: Richie wondered **if***

[or **whether**] *he should wear his green checked suit.* Occasionally you'll need to keep *or not* for emphasis: *Richie wanted to wear the green one,* **whether** *it had a gravy stain* **or not**.

imply/infer. These words are poles apart. To *imply* is to suggest, or to throw out a suggestion; to *infer* is to conclude, or to take in a suggestion. *"You* **imply** *that I'm an idiot," said Stanley. "You* **infer** *correctly," said Blanche.*

in behalf of/on behalf of. The difference may be tiny, but it's worth knowing. *In behalf of* means "for the benefit of" or "in the interest of." *On behalf of* means "in place of" or "as the agent of." *Bertie presented the check* **on behalf of** *the Drones Club, to be used* **in behalf of** *the feebleminded.*

in to/into. Yes, there is a difference! Don't combine *in* and *to* to form *into* just because they happen to land next to each other. *Into* is for entering something (like a room or a profession), for changing the form of something (an ugly duckling, for instance), or for making contact (with a friend or a wall, perhaps). *Get* **into** *the coach before it turns* **into** *a pumpkin, and don't bang* **into** *the door!* Otherwise, use *in to. Bring the guests* **in to** *me, then we'll all go* **in to** *dinner.* (You wouldn't go *into* dinner, unless of course you jumped *into* the soup tureen.) And be careful with *tune* and *turn: I think I'll* **tune in to** *my favorite TV show and* **turn into** *a couch potato.*

Still having a hard time with *into* and *in to*? Here's a trick to help keep them straight. If you can drop the *in* without losing the meaning, the term you want is *in to*. *Bring the guests [**in**] to me, then we'll all go [**in**] to dinner.* (Yes, there's also a difference between *on to* and *onto*, page 105.)

ingenious/ingenuous. Something that's *ingenious* (pronounced in-JEEN-yus) is clever or brilliant; the tip-off is that it has the pronunciation of *genius* built right in. *Ingenuous* (in-JEN-you-us) means frank, candid, unworldly, or innocently open; it's related to *ingénue*, a word for an inexperienced girl. (Calling somebody *disingenuous*— insincere—is a roundabout way of saying he lies.)

lay/lie. To *lay* is to place something; there's always a "something" that's being placed. To *lie* is to recline. *If you're not feeling well, **lay** your tools aside and **lie** down.* (These two get really confusing in the past tense. There's more about *lay* and *lie,* and how to use them in the past, on page 64.)

lend/loan. Only the strictest grammarians now insist that *loan* is the noun and *lend* is the verb, a distinction that is still adhered to in Britain (***Lend** me a pound, there's a good chap*). American usage allows that either *loan* or *lend* may be used as a verb (***Loan** me a few bucks till payday*). To my ears, though, *lend* and *lent* do sound a bit more polished than *loan* and *loaned*.

liable/likely. They're not interchangeable, but they come mighty close sometimes. Use *likely* if you mean probable or expected. Use *liable* if you mean bound by law or obligation (as in *liable for damages*), or exposed to risk or misfortune. *If Madeline goes skating, she's **liable** to fall, and not **likely** to try it again.*

like/as. Which of these is correct? *Homer tripped, [as or **like**] anyone would.* The answer is *as,* because it is followed by a clause, a group of words with both a subject (*anyone*) and a verb (*would*). If no verb follows, choose *like*: *Homer walks **like** a duck.*

Those are the rules, but the ground is shifting. In casual usage, *like* is gaining steadily on *as* (*She tells it **like** it is*), and on its cousins *as if* and *as though,* which are used to introduce clauses that are hypothetical or contrary to fact (*She eats chocolate **like** it's going out of style*).

The informal use of *like* to introduce a clause may be fine in conversation or casual writing, but for those occasions when you want to be grammatically correct, here's how to remember the "*as* comes before a clause" rule: Just think of the notorious old cigarette ad—"*Winston tastes good like a cigarette should*"—and do the opposite. On those more relaxed occasions, do as you like.

like/such as. Which is correct? *Rachel prefers cool colors, [**like** or **such as**] blue, violet, and aqua.* It's a matter of taste—either is acceptable. To my ear, *like* sounds better; *such as* has a more formal air. Of course, there are times when a bit of stiffness is appropriate: "*I've got my reasons for always using **like**,*" said Rufus T. Firefly. "***Such as?***" said Mrs. Teasdale.

loath/loathe. The one without an *e* is an adjective describing somebody who's unwilling or reluctant, and it's usually followed by *to*: *Dmitri is **loath** to eat in Indian restaurants.* The one with an *e* is a verb: *He **loathes** chicken vindaloo.*

may/might. These are tricky. In the present tense, *might* is used rather than *may* to describe an iffier situation. Something that *might* happen is more of a long shot than something that *may* happen. For more, see page 59.

nauseated/nauseous. It's the difference between sick and sickening. You are made sick (*nauseated*) by something sickening (*nauseous*). Never say, *"I'm nauseous."* Even if it is true, it's not something you should admit. *"I'm **nauseated** by that **nauseous** cigar!" said Ethel.*

on to/onto. If you mean on top of or aware of, use *onto*. (*The responsibility shifted **onto** Milo's shoulders. "I'm really **onto** your shenanigans," he said.*) Otherwise, use *on to*: *Hang **on to** your hat.* Sometimes it helps to imagine a word like "ahead" or "along" between them: *Milo drove **on to** Chicago. He was moving **on to** better things.* (Confused about *in to* and *into*? See page 102.)

oral/verbal. They're not the same, though the meanings do overlap. *Oral* means by mouth or by spoken word. *Verbal* means by written or spoken word. That's why *verbal* is so easily misunderstood. What's a *verbal* contract? Written or spoken? It can be either. When it's important to make the distinction, use *oral* when you mean spoken, *written* when you mean written. In the words of Sam Goldwyn: "A verbal contract isn't worth the paper it's written on."

ought/ought to. Which is proper? You'll always be correct if you use *ought to*. Omit *to*, if you wish, in a negative statement: *Children **ought** not take candy from strangers. Pigs **ought** never be allowed in the kitchen.*

overwhelming/overweening. The more familiar *overwhelming* means just what you think it does—too much! *Overweening*, a useful word that we don't see very often, means conceited or pretentious. *The arrogance of that **overweening** little jerk is simply **overwhelming**.*

palate/palette/pallet. Maybe you don't have any trouble telling these apart, but I have to look them up every time. The *palate* is the roof of the mouth, and the word also refers to the sense of taste (the letters spell "a plate"). A *palette*, the board a painter mixes colors on, is also a range of colors. A *pallet* is a rustic bed, usually a makeshift mattress of straw or some other humble material. *Vincent painted his supper, then ate it. Having satisfied his **palate**, he cleaned his **palette** and retired to his **pallet**.*

pore over/pour over. You *pore over* an engrossing book, but it's gross to *pour over* one. *While Charlotte **pored** over a steamy novel, the bathtub **poured over**.*

presume/presumptive/presumptuous. See the discussion of **assume/presume**, page 91.

principal/principle. Still can't keep these straight? A *principal* is a leading figure (the head of a school, for example), and plays a leading, or *principal*, role. A *principle*, on the other hand, is a rule or standard. Here's a memory aid: If you're good in school, the *principal* is your *p-a-l*.

prophecy/prophesy. The *prophecy* (noun) is what's foretold. To *prophesy* (verb) is to foretell. As for pronunciation, *prophecy* ends in a "see," *prophesy* in a "sigh." *Madame Olga charged $50 per **prophecy**, claiming she could **prophesy** fluctuations in the commodities market.*

rack/wrack. Are you *racked* with guilt, or *wracked*? Is tax time nerve-*racking,* or nerve-*wracking*? Are you on the brink of *rack* and ruin, or *wrack* and ruin? Most of the time, you are *racked* (tortured, strained, stretched, punished). Just think of the *rack,* the medieval instrument of torture. If you're *wracked,* on the other hand, you're destroyed—you're *wreckage* on the beach of life (the words *wrack* and *wreck* are related). In sum: *You are **racked** with guilt, you've had a nerve-**racking** time, and you're facing **wrack** and ruin.* You need a less stressful life!

raise/rise. To *raise* is to bring something up; there's always a "something" that's being lifted. To *rise* is to get up. *When they **raise** the flag, we all **rise**.* (There's more about *raise* and *rise,* and how they're used in the past tense, on page 65.)

ravage/ravish. When the ocean liner *Queen Elizabeth* caught fire and burned in Hong Kong harbor, a newspaper in Minnesota heralded the news with this headline: "Queen Elizabeth Ravished." What the headline writer intended was *ravaged,* meaning damaged or destroyed. There's an element of lust in *ravish,* which means to carry off (either by force or by emotion) or to rape. These days we're more likely to use *ravish* in the emotional than in the violent sense. *Though it was **ravaged** by the cleaners, the dress still looked **ravishing***.

regretfully/regrettably. A person who's full of regret is *regretful,* and sighs *regretfully.* A thing that's a cause of regret is *regrettable,* and *regrettably* that's the situation. *Hazel **regretfully** swept up the Ming vase, which **regrettably** had smashed to smithereens.*

reluctant/reticent. These aren't even distant cousins. A *reluctant* person is unwilling, but a *reticent* one is silent. *The **reluctant** bride was **reticent** when asked to say "I do."* By the way, *reticent* comes from the same Latin verb (meaning "to keep silent") as *tacit* (unspoken) and *taciturn* (uncommunicative).

set/sit. To *set* is to place something; there's always a "something" that's being placed. To *sit* is to be seated. *Set the groceries on the counter and sit at the table.* (There's more about *set* and *sit,* and how they're used in the past tense, on page 64.)

spade/spayed. People who confuse these must drive veterinarians crazy. A *spade* is a small, skinny shovel. An altered female dog or cat is *spayed.* To *spade* a garden is to dig it up; to *spay* a cat is to keep her from having kittens. *Ashley took up a **spade** and **spaded** the flower bed, while Melanie took Boots to be **spayed***.

stationary/stationery. If the *stationery* (paper) is *stationary* (fixed or still), you can write on it, and it won't move. (Hint: Both *stationery* and *paper* contain *er.*) "*If you* *haven't become* **stationary,** *Barney, please get up and bring me my* **stationery,**" *said Thelma Lou.*

than/then. Does it make your hair stand on end when someone writes: *"He's taller* **then** *his brother"*? No? Go stand in the corner. *Than* and *then* are similar only in the way they sound. If you're comparing or contrasting things, use *than,* as in *more* **than** or *less* **than.** If one thing follows or results from another, use *then* (as in, *Look,* **then** *leap*). *The next morning, Paolo was sicker* **than** *a dog. He took some aspirin,* **then** *went back to bed. "If gin disagrees with you,* **then** *avoid it," said Francesca.* For advice on *than* when it comes before a pronoun (*I, me, he, she,* etc.), see page 12.

though/although. These are interchangeable, except in two cases, when only *though* will do:

- in the phrases *as though* or *even though;*
- when it's used to mean "however." *Madame Olga predicted it would rain in Brazil; it didn't,* **though.**

tortuous/torturous. The first means winding, crooked, full of turns. The second, as you may suspect from its root word, *torture,* means painful. *On the* **tortuous** *drive through the mountains, Jake developed a* **torturous** *headache.*

try and/try to. The proper phrase is *try to,* as in: *"***Try to** *eat your soup without slurping," said Nancy.* But *try and* is gaining acceptance in spoken and informal use, and seems appropriate when there's an added note of defiance or stiffening of resolve: *"***Try and** *make me," said Sluggo.*

until/till. Either of these is correct, but not "til." And using *up* or *since* with *until* is unnecessary. *Until* [not *Up until*] *recently, Sluggo's tie was spotless.*

will/would. These are often confused when paired with other verbs. Use *will* after a verb in the present tense (*He says he will*) and *would* after a verb in the past (*He said he would*). For more, see page 75.

Use It (Right) or Lose It

both. The pair (of people, things, ideas, etc.) following *both* should have the same accessories:

If one has a preposition (*as, by, for, to,* and so on), so must the other: *Phineas has proposed both to Mary and to Laura.* Or: *Phineas has proposed to both Mary and Laura.*

If one has a verb (an action word), so must the other: *His attentions both pleased them and flattered them.* Or: *His attentions were both pleasing and flattering.*

comprise. It means include or contain. *Vladimir's butterfly collection comprises several rare specimens.* Avoid *comprised of.* You wouldn't say "included of," would you? The *of* is correct, however, in *composed of* and *consists of.*

couple. It takes *of: Elaine considers them a couple of idiots.* Not: *Elaine considers them a couple idiots.* Similarly, *plenty of, type of, variety of, breed of, kind of: What breed of dog is he?*

NOTE: Sometimes *couple* is singular and sometimes it's plural. See pages 25 and 53.

depend. It takes *on.* "Well," said Buster, "that **depends on** what [not **depends what**] you mean by housebroken."

due to. When you want to be on your very best grammatical behavior, use *due to* only if you mean "caused by" or "resulting from": *The damage was **due to** moths.* In recent years, dictionaries have come to accept a looser usage, meaning "because of" or "on account of": *Richie threw the suit away **due to** the hole.* But be warned that some find this grating, especially at the front of a sentence: ***Due to** the hole, Richie threw the suit away.*

equally as. Forget the *as: Ken and Midge are **equally** obnoxious.* Or: *Ken is **as** obnoxious **as** Midge.*

forbid. Use *forbid* with *to,* never with *from: I **forbid** you **to** spit.* (Not: *I **forbid** you **from** spitting.*) As an alternative, you can use *forbid* with an *ing* word alone: *I **forbid** spitting.* For more about *forbid,* see page 63.

graduated. There are three rights and a wrong:
Right: *Moose **graduated from** college.*
Right: *Moose **was graduated from** college.*
Right: *The college **graduated** Moose.*
Wrong: *Moose **graduated** college.*

hardly. Don't use *hardly* with a negative verb, as in: *She can't **hardly** see without her glasses. Hardly* is already a negative word, and you don't need two of them. Either of these is correct: *She **can hardly** see without her glasses.* Or: *She can't see without her glasses.*

hardly / scarcely / no sooner. Watch your *when*s and *than*s with these. Use *when* with *hardly* and *scarcely*: *We had **hardly** begun to cook **when** the smoke alarm went off.* Or: *We had **scarcely** begun to cook **when** the smoke alarm went off.* Use *than* with *no sooner*: ***No sooner** had we begun to cook **than** the smoke alarm went off.*

hence. Like its cousin *whence* (see below), *hence* has a built-in "from"—it means "from here" or "from now." So using "from" with *hence* is redundant. *"My birthday is three days **hence**," said Corky, "and I could really use a dehumidifier."* Another meaning of *hence* is "thus": *It's damp, **hence** the mildew.*

HIV. This is the AIDS virus; the letters stand for "human immunodeficiency virus." Since *virus* is already part of the name, it's redundant to repeat it. *He's doing research on HIV* (not "on the HIV virus").

inside of. Drop the *of*: *Penelope keeps her hankie **inside** her glove.*

kudos. This is a singular noun meaning praise or glory (*Bart won **kudos** for his skateboarding skill*), not a plural form of some imaginary "kudo." Show me one kudo and I'll eat it.

likely (with a verb). When you use *likely* to describe an action, don't use it all by itself; precede it with *very, quite,* or *most*: *Nathan will **quite likely** lose his shirt at the track* (not "will likely lose"). If you prefer, use *is **likely** to* instead:

Nathan is likely to lose a bundle, and Miss Adelaide is likely to kill him.

myriad. It originally meant "ten thousand," but *myriad* now means "numerous" or "a great number of." (*Lulu has myriad freckles.*) Avoid the redundant "myriads" or "a myriad of."

oblivious. It's better with *of,* not *to. Olivia was oblivious of her liver.*

only. Aside from conversational or casual language, don't use *only* in place of *but* or *except: I would go to Paris, but* [not *only*] *I'm broke.* For more on *only,* see page 122.

prohibit. Use *prohibit* with *from,* never with *to: The rules prohibit you from spitting.* (Not: *The rules prohibit you to spit.*) As an alternative, you can follow *prohibit* with an *ing* word alone: *The rules prohibit spitting.* For more about *prohibit,* see page 63.

whence. Not *from whence.* The "from" is built in. *Whence* means "from where." (*Go back whence you came, brigand!*) The same is true of *hence* and *thence*: use them alone, since "from" is implied. Their cousins *whither, hither,* and *thither* have "to" built in. If you must use a grizzled old word, treat it with respect. (See **hence** above.)

whether or not. You can usually ditch *or not: Phoebe knows whether Holden is telling the truth.* (See if/**whether,** page 101.)

while. The classic meaning is "during the time that": *Doc whistles while he works.* But *while* has also gained acceptance as a substitute for *although* or *whereas* at the beginning of a sentence or clause: *While Grumpy can whistle, he prefers not to.*

NOTE: If you use *while* in place of *although,* be sure there's no chance it could be misunderstood to mean "during the time that." You could leave the impression that unlikely things were happening at the same time, as in: *While Dopey sleeps late, he enjoys vigorous exercise.* Only if Dopey is a sleepwalker! For how to use *a while* and *awhile,* see page 120.

You're Getting Warmer: Spelling and Saying It Right

accommodate. It has two *c*'s and two *m*'s. *"I believe I can accommodate you, even without a reservation,"* said Mr. Fawlty.

advertise/advertisement/advertising. Here in the United States, each of these has an *s* (the preference in Britain is to use a *z*). *When Jack got his job at the advertising agency, he didn't advertise the fact that he'd never written an advertisement.*

all-round. *Shep is a good all-round dog.* All-round is better than *all-around,* in the sense of complete or rounded. This is a case where it's better to round off the word.

arctic. Not "artic" (don't forget the middle *c*). The lower-case *arctic* means very cold. The capitalized *Arctic* means the region. And it's *Antarctica*, not "Antarica" (a common misspelling). *The **Arctic** expedition reached the North Pole. Next year's goal, **Antarctica**, is in the opposite direction.* I was once astonished to see a big sign from Coors advertising a frosty beverage called Artic Ice. Never trust anything you read on the side of a bus.

artifact. Not "artefact." That's with an *i*, not an *e*: *"An 1840 saxophone is a rare **artifact**," said Lisa.*

desiccated. One *s*, two *c*'s. *"A raisin is simply a **desiccated** grape," said Uncle Fester.*

ecstasy. Two *s*'s (not "ecstacy"; and there's no *x*). *Miranda was in **ecstasy**.*

embarrass. Two *r*'s and two *s*'s. *Spock was not **embarrassed** by his pointy ears.*

fulfill. One *l* in the middle, two at the end. *Did Paulie **fulfill** his obligation?*

guerrilla. Two *r*'s and two *l*'s. *Che raised a **guerrilla** army.* (It's the ape that's a *gorilla*.)

harass. One *r* and two *s*'s. As for pronunciation, you may accent either syllable, although the preference on this side of the Atlantic is to stress the second. *"Wally, stop **harassing** your brother," said Ward.*

hyperbole. It is not pronounced like the name of a sporting event, the Hyper Bowl; it's high-PER-buh-lee. It means exaggeration or overstatement. *Buster's claim that his dog could read was **hyperbole**.*

NOTE: If you've seen **hyper/hypo** (page 101), you may wonder whether there's such a word as *hypobole*. As a matter of fact, there is (it means something like "suggestion"), but I've never heard anybody use it.

indispensable. It ends in *able*, not *ible*. *"Nick, you're **indispensable**," said Nora.*

irresistible. It ends in *ible*, not *able*. I wish there were an easy way to tell the *ible*s from the *able*s, but there isn't. You're at the mercy of your dictionary. *"Nora, you're **irresistible**," said Nick.*

judgment. No *e* after the *g*. (The same goes for *acknowledgment*, but not *knowledgeable*.) *"I never make snap **judgments**," said Solomon.*

lightning. Flash! There's no *e* in *lightning*, the kind that leaves us thunderstruck: *A bolt of **lightning** split the sky.* The word with an *e* (*lightening*) comes from *lighten*: *I'll bet she's **lightening** her hair.*

marvelous. One *l*. (The British spell it with two, but pay no attention.) *"Gertrude, that's a **marvelous** haircut!" said Alice.*

memento. It's not spelled—or pronounced—"momento." Think of the word remem*b*rance. *The embroidered pillow was a **memento** of Niagara Falls.*

minuscule. It's not spelled—or, again, pronounced—"miniscule." Think of *minus* as the root, not *mini*. *Barbie's accessories are **minuscule**.*

nuclear. Pronounce it NOO-klee-ur (not NOO-kyoo-lur). *"My business is **nuclear** energy," said Homer.*

rarefied. It's spelled with one *i*, not "rarified." (If in doubt, think of *rare*.) *McCoy feared that the rarefied air in the Enterprise was enervating the crew.* (If you don't know what *enervating* means, see page 83.)

restaurateur. Notice that there's no *n* (and don't believe dictionaries or spell-checkers that tell you there is). The root is a word meaning "restore." The *restaurateur* (the person who restores you) runs the *restaurant* (where you go to get restored). *When Apu became a restaurateur, he called his restaurant Curry in a Hurry.*

skillful. Two *l*'s in the middle, one at the end. *Tex was skillful with a lasso.*

sprightly. The word meaning energetic has a *gh*; it's not "spritely": *Ed and Trixie were feeling sprightly.* Someone who's like a sprite, a little imaginary creature resembling a pixie or an elf, is *spritelike. Ed looked spritelike in his leprechaun costume.*

straitjacket/straitlaced. There's no *gh* in either—not "straightjacket" or "straightlaced." *Straitlaced people who go over the edge may find themselves in straitjackets.* The word *strait* is from the Latin *strictus*, which means "constricted" or "tight." *Straight*, from an Anglo-Saxon word for "stretch," means uncurved. The word you run across in geography, by the way, is *strait*, referring to a tight waterway: the *Strait* of Gibraltar, the Bering *Strait*.

toward. No final *s* ("towards"), although that's how they say it in Britain. Similarly, in American English, standard practice is not to add a final *s* to *forward, backward, up-ward, onward, downward,* and so on. *George and Kramer were last seen heading* **toward** *the buffet.*

weird. It's spelled *ei*, not *ie. "You're looking particularly* **weird** *this evening, Morticia, my love," said Gomez.*

"Seedy" Endings

Words that end with a "seed" sound are notoriously hard to spell. It helps to keep in mind that all but four end with *cede*. Three end with *ceed*, and only one ends with *sede*.

- **cede:** accede, antecede, cede, concede, intercede, precede, recede, secede (and others)
- **ceed:** exceed, proceed, succeed
- **sede:** supersede

One Word or Two?

all ready/already. They're not the same. *All ready* means prepared; *already* means previously. *Carrie and Samantha are **all ready** to boogie; in fact, they've **already** started.*

all together/altogether. They differ. *All together* means collectively—all at once or all in one place: *Bertie's aunts were **all together** in the living room. Altogether* means in sum or entirely: *Altogether there were four of them. Bertie was **altogether** defeated.*

any more/anymore. Use *any more* if you mean any additional; use *anymore* if you mean nowadays or any longer. *Shep won't be chasing **any more** cars. He doesn't get around much **anymore**.*

any one/anyone. If you can substitute *anybody,* then the single word *anyone* is correct; if not, use two words, *any one.* **Anyone** *can fool Lumpy.* **Any one** *of his friends is smarter than he is.* (See also **every one/everyone** below.)

any place/anyplace. One word is acceptable if you mean *anywhere* (though *anywhere* is usually better). If in doubt, use two. *I can afford to live **anyplace**, but I can't live in **any place** that doesn't accept pets.*

any time/anytime. Use two words if you mean "any amount of time," one if you mean "whenever." *The boss will see you **anytime** she has **any time**.*

any way/anyway. It's one word if you mean "in any case." Otherwise, use two words, *any way*. Never "anyways." *I don't know of **any way** to visit the dungeons without bumping into Snape. You wouldn't want to see them, **anyway**.*

awhile/a while. These are often confused when they're written. *Awhile* means "for a time"; "for" is part of the meaning and shouldn't be added. *A while* means "a period of time." *Heloise rested **awhile**; she put her feet up and dozed for **a while***. (For how to use *while*, see page 113.)

every day/everyday. We mix them up daily (or *every day*). The single word, *everyday*, is an adjective. It describes a thing, so it can usually be found right in front of a noun: *"I just love my **everyday** diamonds," said Magda.* The time expression *every day* is two words: *"That's why you wear them **every day**," said Eva.*

every one/everyone. If you can substitute *everybody*, then the single word *everyone* is correct; if not, use two words, *every one*. ***Everyone** fears Dagmar's children. **Every one** of them is a little terror.*

Detour—Dangerous
Construction Ahead

all . . . not/not all. Many sentences that are built around *all . . . not* face backward. Use *not all* instead: *Not*

all Swedes are blond. To say, **All** Swedes are **not** blond, is to say that not a single Swede has golden hair.

as bad or worse than. Stay away from this kind of sentence: *Opie's math is* ***as bad or worse than*** *his English.* Do you see what's wrong with it? Well, there are two kinds of comparisons going on, *as bad as* and *worse than*. When you telescope them into *as bad or worse than*, you lose an *as*. Putting it back in (*Opie's math is* ***as bad as or worse than*** *his English*) is correct but cumbersome. A better idea is to put the rear end of the comparison (*or worse*) at the end of the sentence: *Opie's math is* ***as bad as*** *his English,* ***or worse***. (Another way to end the sentence is *if not worse*.)

as good or better than. This is a variation on the previous theme. It's better to split up the comparison: *Harry's broom is* ***as good as*** *Malfoy's,* ***or better***. (Another way to end it is *if not better*.)

as much or more than. Here's another variation on *as bad or worse than* (see above). Don't use this phrase all at once; split it up: *Otis loves bourbon* ***as much as*** *rye,* ***or more***. (Another ending is *if not more*.)

See **one of the . . . if not the** below, for a way out of another common trap.

either . . . or. Think of the elements joined by *either* and *or* as the two sides of a coin. Make sure the sides are even. If what follows *either* has a subject and a verb (is a clause, in other words), what follows *or* should, too: ***Either Kenny did*** *or* ***he didn't***. If what follows *either* starts with a preposition (a word that "positions," or locates, other words in the sentence), then what follows *or* should, too: *Kenny is **either** at school **or** in trouble.* If what follows *either* is an adjective (a word that characterizes something), then so is what follows *or*: *Truant officers are **either** spiteful **or** misguided.* In short, the two sides of the coin, the *either* and *or* parts, must match grammatically—subject with subject, verb with verb, preposition with preposition, adjective with adjective, and so on. If the sides aren't equal, you can often fix the problem by moving *either* a few words over. So this blunder, ***Either** Mrs. McCormick is angry **or** amused,* becomes *Mrs. McCormick is **either** angry **or** amused.*

> **NOTE:** Several other pairs should be treated as flip sides of the same coin: *neither . . . nor; not only . . . but also; both . . . and.* As with *either . . . or,* they may take some arranging; all require that the two sides match.

one of the . . . if not the. Here's another corner you can avoid backing yourself into: *Jordan was **one of the** best, **if not the** best, player on the team.* Oops! Can you hear what's wrong? The sentence should read correctly even if the second half of the comparison (*if not the best*) is removed; but without it you've got: *Jordan was one of the best player on the team.* One of the best *player*? Better to put the second half of the comparison at the end of the sentence: *Jordan was **one of the** best players on the team, **if not the** best.*

only. This slippery word—meaning "alone," "solely," or

"and no other"—can be found almost anywhere in a sentence, even where it doesn't belong. To put *only* in its place, make sure it goes right before the word or phrase you want to single out as the lone wolf. Take this sentence as an example: *The butler says he saw the murder.* By inserting *only* in various places, you can give the sentence many different meanings. Keep your eye on the underlined words—those are the wolves being singled out of the pack:

- *Only the butler says he saw the murder.* (The butler, and no one else, says he saw the murder.)
- *The butler only says he saw the murder.* (The butler says, but can't prove, he saw the murder.)
- *The butler says only he saw the murder.* (The butler says he, and no one else, saw it.)
- *The butler says he only saw the murder.* (He saw—but didn't hear—the murder.)
- *The butler says he saw only the murder.* (He saw just the murder, and nothing else.)

Remember: *Only* the lonely! It's easy to slip *only* into a sentence carelessly, so get into the habit of using it right in front of the word you want to single out.

NOTE: The whole point of putting *only* in its place is to make yourself understood. In the examples above, the various locations of *only* make a big difference. But in informal writing and conversation, if no one's likely to mistake your meaning, it's fine to put *only* where it seems most natural—usually in front of the verb: *I'm* **only** *going to say this once; This food can* **only** *be called swill*. The more grammatically correct versions—*I'm going to say this* **only** *once; This food can be called* **only** *swill*—only sound unnatural.

reason . . . is because. Here's a redundancy for you, a wording that seems to repeat itself: *The* **reason** *Rex stayed home* **is because** *robbers tied him up*. Can you hear the echo effect? *Because* means "for the reason that," so the example says, in effect: *The* **reason** *Rex stayed home is* **for the reason that** *robbers tied him up*. Use one or the other, not both: *The* **reason** *Rex stayed home is that robbers tied him up*. Or: *Rex stayed home* **because** *robbers tied him up*.

Overwriters Anonymous

at this time. A bit overstuffed, no? (*Dr. Melfi has no openings* **at this time**.) Why not just *now*? (*Dr. Melfi has no openings now*.)

if and when. Wordy people are very fond of this phrase (*I'll punch out his lights,* **if and when** *I see him*). Use either *if* or *when*; you seldom need both.

in order to. Unless there's some need for special emphasis, drop *in order* and simply use *to*: *"I work* **to** *live, and I live* **to** *boogie," said Tallulah*.

unless or until. (*"I'm not talking, **unless or until** I see my lawyer!" said Mr. Bluster.*) One or the other will usually do, unless or until you're getting paid by the word.

Sensibility and Sense

gender. Let's hope *gender* never replaces *sex*. An old and durable word, *sex* (from the Latin *sexus*) has long meant either of the two divisions—male and female—that characterize living things. (*Annie Oakley was a credit to her sex.*) By extension it has also come to refer to the sexual act. *Gender,* a grammatical term for "kind," describes the ways some languages categorize nouns and pronouns by sex (masculine, feminine, or neuter). Perhaps it was inevitable that as we began speaking more openly about sex and sex roles, some people would feel a need for a more neutral word to refer to the Great Divide, one with no taint of the act itself. *Gender* seemed to fit the bill. (*Little Emily plays with dolls of both **genders**.*) Well, this horse, too, is out of the barn. But to my ear, *gender* sounds prudish as an alternative to *sex*. Until a better word comes along, I'll stick with the three-letter original. If *sex* was good enough for Jane Austen ("Miss de Bourgh is far superior to the handsomest of her sex"), it's good enough for me.

-man/-woman/-person. Speaking of sex, here's something else to think about. For a thousand years, give or take, the word *man* has done double duty, as a term for both the male of the species and the species as a whole. In the last half-century or so, sensibilities have changed, and this state of affairs now strikes many people as lopsided. *Man* and its variations no longer seem appropriate as catch-alls, especially when we refer to women: *When Cynthia was **chairman**, she provided most of the **manpower**.* See what I mean? If you know a person's sex, why not call her a *chairwoman* or him a *chairman*? If you don't know, there's always an alternative, like *head* instead of *chairman, press officer* instead of *spokesman, firefighter* instead of *fireman, representative* instead of *congressman,* and so on. Of course, there are always the *person* words (*chairperson, spokesperson, councilperson, businessperson, ombudsperson*). Personally, I find them clunky and self-conscious. Then there's *chair,* a solution inspired, perhaps, by the precedent of *table* as a parliamentary term. I'm in the minority on this one, but I think of a chair as an article of furniture. Feel free to disagree.

Department of Hot Air

dialogue. Can we *dialogue*? No, thanks. I'd rather talk, chat, gossip, speak, converse, exchange ideas, or shoot the breeze. Some people prefer to *dialogue,* or to *have a dia-*

logue. Don't talk to them. (For a related cliché, see **mean-ingful dialogue**, page 174.)

impact. The kind of person who uses language as a sledge-hammer is likely to use *impact* as a verb meaning affect. (*"The third-quarter loss will impact our earnings projections for the year," said Daddy Warbucks.*) If you don't want to give the rest of the world a headache, use *impact* only as a noun. (*"Will this have any impact on my allowance?" asked Annie.*)

interface. People who like to *dialogue* also like to *interface.* By this they mean interact, or work together. Don't work with them.

monies. This is how a bureaucrat says *money.* *"But where will these monies come from?" asked Councilman Windbag.*

paradigm. It masquerades as a two-dollar word, but it's really worth only about twenty cents. A *paradigm* (the *g* is silent: PAIR-a-dime) is simply a pattern or example. It's not a standard of perfection (that's a *paragon*). Still, homely old *paradigm,* along with its cousin *paradigmatic* (here the *g* is sounded), has become the darling of those who like to dress up ordinary ideas in technicalities. *"Our ad campaign has a paradigmatic resonance," said Mr. Palaver.*

parameter. There's nothing like a scientific word to lend an air of authority to a weak sentence. (*"Let us review the parameters of the issue," said Senator Blowhard.*) That's how a word like *parameter* (a mathematical term for a type of arbitrary constant or independent variable) worms its way into the Official Overwriters' Vocabulary. Don't let it get into yours. Weak writers use *parameter* to mean a boundary, a characteristic, a component, an element, a feature, an ingredient, a part, a perimeter, a quality, or a requirement. When a word is used for too many things, it ends up meaning nothing. Unless you know an independent variable from an arbitrary constant, stay away from *parameter*.

say. You've *said* it before, and you'll *say* it again, because if there's a word that *says* it all, surely it's the verb *say*. (*"I love you," he said.*) So why do some writers avoid it? The problem with *say* is that it's just too simple and clear and straightforward for many people. Why *say* something, when you can declare, assert, expostulate, whine, exclaim, groan, peal, breathe, cry, explain, or asseverate it? I'm all for variety and freshness of expression, but let's not go overboard. As Freud said, sometimes a cigar is just a cigar.

transpire. This is how a stuffed shirt says *happen* or *occur* or *take place*: *"Let us review exactly what **transpired** at the First Continental Congress,"* said Professor Jawbone.

unprecedented. *Judge Hearsay's action was **unprecedented**.* Oh yeah? Very few things are unprecedented. Don't use this word to mean unusual, uncommon, odd, unexpected, rare, exceptional, curious, irregular, offbeat, or surprising. No matter how extraordinary something sounds to you, there's probably a precedent for it. *Mr. Scrooge's generosity was **unprecedented**—for him.*

You Call That a Word?

ahold. A horror! Either it's two words (*"Gal, you've really got **a hold** on me," said Roy*), or it's simply *hold* (*"For heaven's sake, Roy, get **hold** of yourself," said Dale*).

ain't. It's still misbehavin'. Not: *"I **ain't** hanging up my six-guns just yet," said Shane.*

alot. Ouch! It's two words: *a lot. He hasn't done his friends **a lot** of good.*

alright. No, *alright* is not *all right*—it's all wrong! *"**All right**, I'll let you whitewash the fence!" said Tom.*

anywheres. Never. It's *anywhere. "The aliens could be almost **anywhere**," said Ripley.*

being that. This clunker is sometimes used as an alternative to *since* or *because*: ***Being that** he was hungry, he ate a piece of Mildred's fruitcake.* It may squeak by in conversation (not with me, please!) but should be avoided in writing. *Being as* and *being as how* are just as bad. They aren't felonies, but neither is snoring at the ballet. (The same goes for *seeing that, seeing as,* and *seeing as how*.)

complected. No; the word traditionally favored is *complexioned. After years of riding the range with no sunscreen, Yosemite Sam was dark-**complexioned**.*

dove (for **dived**). *Dived* is still the preferred past tense for what Esther Williams did off a diving board, but *dove* is surfacing more and more. In writing, stick to *dived*; in conversation, especially if it's casual, you can get by with *dove* (though I'd rather see it sink). *With the swamp before him and an angry rhino at his heels, Indiana dived into the murky waters.*

irregardless. This isn't a word—it's a crime in progress! The word you want is *regardless.* (*Dick and Nicole do as they like, regardless of the consequences.*) Irrespective of what you hear and read, there is no such word as *irregardless.*

orientate. The extra syllable is ugly and unnecessary, though not a hanging offense. *Orient* is sufficient. *Santiago tried to orient himself without a compass.*

preventative. The extra syllable isn't wrong, but it's unnecessary. Use *preventive. Always wear sunscreen as a preventive measure.*

seeing that. See **being that** above.

Plug Ugly

Words are easy to stretch. Just add *ly* to a word like *neat* and you end up with *neatly*: *It's a neat trick to pack a suitcase neatly.* What could be neater?

But not all words like having *ly* tacked on to them, especially if they already end in *ly,* like *ugly, friendly, surly,* and *jolly.* Sure, the dictionary says we can use lame adverbs like *uglily, friendlily, surlily,* and *jollily,* but nobody says we have to.

If a word doesn't want to be stretched out of shape, don't force it.

Et Cetera

a/an. Sometimes it's the little things that give us away. For instance, we all know the rule about using *an* in front of words that begin with vowels (*a, e, i, o, u*), and *a* in front of those starting with consonants (letters with a "hard" sound, like *b, c, d, f, g, h,* and so on). But what happens when *h* sounds like a vowel or *u* sounds like a consonant? A pair of handy rules:

- Use *a* (not *an*) in front of words that start with these sounds: a "sounded" *h* (the *ha-ha* variety, as in *history, horror, hotel*); a "long" *u* (the *yew* variety, as in *university, utopia, eulogy, European*).
- Use *an* in front of words that start with these sounds: a "silent" *h* (*hour, honor, herbal*); a "short" *u* (*uncle, umbrella, undertaker*).

and/or. This ugly wrinkle (*Tubby, would you like apple pie and/or ice cream?*) can be smoothed out: *Tubby, would you like apple pie, ice cream, or both?*

at. Avoid using it unnecessarily with *where*, as in *Where is Silvio at? The at* is understood, so all you need is *Where is Silvio?* Understood?

but. It's common practice to use *but* to mean *nothing but* or *only*—just be careful not to get tangled in negatives, since *but* in these cases already has a negative sense built in. *Tom **is but** a boy.* Not: *Tom **isn't but** a boy.*

*Aunt Polly **weighs but** 105 pounds.* Not: *Aunt Polly doesn't **weigh but** 105 pounds.*

> **NOTE:** Avoid using *help but,* as in: *Huck **can't help but** look silly in those pants.* Drop the *but* and use the *ing* form: *Huck **can't help** looking silly in those pants.*

etc. Since this abbreviation (it stands for *et cetera*) means "and others," it's redundant to say or write "and etc." It's even worse to use "etc., etc." (*A conscientious groupie knows all the members of a band: drummer, lead guitar, rhythm, bass, **etc.***) And by the way, if you're one of those people who pronounce it ek-SET-ra, shame on you. There's no *k* sound.

of. Don't use it if you don't need it. *Paulie says his new TV fell off **of** a truck. The missing warranty is not that big **of** a problem.* Whack the *of*: *Paulie says his new TV fell off a truck. The missing warranty is not that big a problem.* (For exceptions, see page 191.)

Chapter 6

Comma Sutra

The Joy of Punctuation

An editor I know at *The New York Times* once received a gift from a writer friend. It was the tip of a lead pencil, broken off and wrapped up and presented along with a card that said, "A gross of commas, to be used liberally throughout the year as needed." Now, that writer understood the gift of punctuation!

When you talk, your voice, with its pauses, stresses, rises, and falls, shows how you intend your words to fit together. When you write, punctuation marks are the road signs (stop, go, yield, slow, detour) that guide the reader, and you wouldn't be understood without them.

If you don't believe me, try making sense out of this pile of words:

Who do you think I saw the other day the Dalai Lama said my aunt Minnie.

There are at least two possibilities:

- *"Who do you think I saw the other day?"* the Dalai Lama said. *"My aunt Minnie."*
- *"Who do you think I saw the other day? The Dalai Lama!"* said my aunt Minnie.

(I know, I know. I've taken liberties with *who* and *whom*. You can, too, in conversation and informal writing. See the chapter on pronouns, page 9.)

Punctuation isn't some subtle, arcane concept that's hard to manage and that probably won't make much of a difference one way or another. It's not subtle, it's not difficult, and it can make all the difference in the world.

The Living End: The Period (.)

The period is the red light at the end of a sentence. When you reach the period, it's all over. Whatever thought you were trying to convey has been delivered. A straightforward sentence that states rather than asks or exclaims something starts with a capital letter and ends with a period.

But what if there's a dot there already, as when a sentence ends with an ellipsis (. . .) or an abbreviation that has periods (A.M., for example)? And what if a sentence has a smaller sentence within it? Here's what you do:

- If a sentence ends with an abbreviation that has a final period, don't add another period: *As a new immigrant, Apu's nephew felt welcome in the U.S.* (More and more abbreviations, like MD, are losing their dots these days, so check your dictionary for updates.)

- If a sentence ends in an ellipsis (three dots that indicate an omission), put a period first to show that the sentence is over: *"You'd like to borrow fifty dollars?" said Apu. He recalled the old saying, Neither a borrower nor a lender be. . . .*

But if you want to emphasize a deliberate trailing off, you may omit the period. End the sentence with a space, then the three dots: *"Well . . ."*

- If a sentence concludes with the title of a work that ends in a question mark or an exclamation point, don't add a final period: *Liz gained twenty pounds for* Who's Afraid of Virginia Woolf? *We couldn't get seats to* Oklahoma!

- If a sentence has a smaller sentence within it (surrounded by dashes or parentheses), don't use a period to end the "inside" sentence: *When Apu made him an offer—"I could use some help around the store"—he accepted.*

NOTE: This last point doesn't apply to question marks or exclamation points: *Apu criticized his nephew's manners ("Speak up! How are the customers supposed to hear you?") and his grooming ("Do you call that a beard?").*

Uncommonly Useful:
The Comma (,)

There's nothing much to punctuating a sentence, really, be-yond a little comma sense. Get the commas right, and the rest will fall into place.

Yeah, yeah, I hear you saying. What's a comma or two—or three? How can something so small, so innocuous, be impor-tant? Well, that attitude can get you tossed into grammatical purgatory. You don't believe it? Take a look:

Cora claimed Frank planned the murder.

Without commas, the finger of guilt points to Frank. But add a pair of commas, and Cora becomes the suspect:

Cora, claimed Frank, planned the murder.

Here's another pair of examples with completely different meanings:

Augie quit saying he was looking for another job.

Augie quit, saying he was looking for another job.

In the first sentence, Augie quit talking; in the second, he quit his job.

The lesson: Don't take commas for granted. They're like yellow traffic lights. If you ignore one, you could be in for a bumpy ride.

Most problems with commas have to do with dividing a sentence into parts—larger parts like clauses (each with its own subject and verb), or smaller ones like items in a series. Commas are also used to interrupt a sentence and insert another thought. Here's how to get out of some of the most common comma complications.

LONG AND SHORT DIVISION

• Use a comma to separate clauses (big chunks of a sentence) joined by *and* or *but*. *Tina hadn't left the city in months, and by Friday she was climbing the walls.* If there's no *and* or *but* in between, use a semicolon instead: *Tina hadn't left the city in months; by Friday she was climbing the walls.*

• Use commas to separate a series of things or actions. *She packed a toothbrush, a hair dryer, her swimsuit, and her teddy bear. She finished packing, paid some bills, ate a few Oreos, and watered the plants.*

NOTE: The final comma in those two series, the one just before *and,* can be left out. It's a matter of taste. But since its absence can sometimes change your meaning, and since there's no harm in leaving it in, my advice is to stick with using the final comma.

AS I WAS SAYING

• Use commas before and after the names of people you're talking to: *"Good-bye, Mom. Dad, be good,"* she said, and hung up the phone. You can skip the comma before the name if all that precedes it is *and* (*"And Mom, don't worry"*) or *but* (*"But Dad, you promised"*).

● Use commas before or after a quotation: *"Let's see,"* *said Tina.* Or: *Tina said, "Let's see."* But don't use a comma after a quotation that ends with an exclamation point or a question mark: *"Have I forgotten anything?" she wondered. "Sunscreen!" she exclaimed.*

LET ME INTERRUPT

● Use a comma after an introductory phrase if a pause is intended: *As usual, she checked to make sure the stove was turned off. Of course, it always was. You see, Tina was a bit compulsive.*

● Use commas around an aside—information that could just as well go in parentheses: *Her upstairs neighbor, the one without the tattoos, promised to collect her mail.*

● Use commas around a *which* clause: *The airport bus, which was usually on time, never came.* You need only the first comma if the clause comes at the end: *So she took a taxi, which cost her an arm and a leg.*

But don't use commas around *that* clauses: *The bus that she had planned to take never came, so she grabbed the first taxi that she saw.*

For more on *which* and *that*, see page 3.

Semi-Avoidance: The Unloved Semicolon (;)

The semicolon is one of the most useful but least used punctuation marks. For whatever reason, many of us avoid it. Maybe it intimidates us; it shouldn't. (See, wasn't that easy?) If a comma is a yellow light and a period is a red light, the semicolon is a flashing red—one of those lights you drive through after a brief pause. It's for times when you want something stronger than a comma but not quite so final as a period. Here's when to use it.

- Use a semicolon to separate clauses when there's no *and* in between: *Andy's toupee flew off his head; it sailed into the distance.*

- Use semicolons to separate items in a series when there's already a comma in one or more of the items: *Fred's favorite things were his robe, a yellow chenille number from Barneys; his slippers; his overstuffed chair, which had once been his father's; murder mysteries, especially those by Sue Grafton; and single-malt Scotch.*

Let Me Introduce You:
The Colon (:)

Think of the colon as a traffic cop, or punctuation's master of ceremonies. Use it to present something: a statement, a series, a quotation, or instructions. But remember that a colon stops the flow of traffic. Use one only if you want to step on the brake. Keep these guidelines in mind.

● Use a colon instead of a comma, if you wish, to introduce a quotation. *I said to him: "Harry, please pick up a bottle of wine on your way over. But don't be obsessive about it."* Many people prefer to introduce a longer quotation with a colon instead of a comma.

● Use a colon to introduce a list, if what comes before the colon could be a small sentence in itself (it has both a subject and a verb). *Harry brought three wines: a Bordeaux, a Beaujolais, and a Burgundy.*

● Don't use a colon to separate a verb from the rest of the sentence, as this example does. *In Harry's shopping bag were: a Bordeaux, a Beaujolais, and a Burgundy.* If you don't need a colon, why use one? *In Harry's shopping bag were a Bordeaux, a Beaujolais, and a Burgundy.*

NOTE: If what comes after the colon is a complete sentence, you may start it with a capital or a lowercase letter. I use a capital when I want to be more emphatic: *My advice was this: Bring only one next time.* (This is a matter of taste, and opinions differ. Whatever your choice, be consistent.)

Huh?
The Question Mark (?)

The question mark is the raised eyebrow at the end of a sentence. It's used with a question, of course, but also to show skepticism or surprise. (*"Lost? My luggage got lost on a direct flight?"*) Here are some of the most common questions about questions.

• What do you do when a sentence has a series of questions? This gets an either/or answer.

You can put the question mark at the very end: *Would Tina have to buy a new hair dryer, toothbrush, swimsuit?*

Or, for emphasis, you can put a question mark after each item (you don't need capital letters for each item, since it's still one sentence): *Would Tina have to buy a new hair dryer? toothbrush? swimsuit?*

• How do you introduce a question within a longer sentence? The simplest way is to use a comma and start the question with a capital letter. *The question was, How long should she wait for her luggage?*

The same is true if the question is a quotation: Introduce it with a comma. *Tina cried, "What next?"*

But if the introduction is a complete sentence, especially if it's a long one, a colon works better. *The question she asked herself was this: How long should she wait for her baggage?*

● What comes after a question mark? If the sentence continues after the question, don't use a comma after the question mark. *What will I do without my hair dryer? she asked herself.* "*What more can go wrong?" she said to the ticket agent.*

The Silent Scream: The Exclamation Point (!)

The exclamation point is like the horn on your car—use it only when you have to. A chorus of exclamation points says two things about your writing: First, you're not confident that what you're saying is important, so you need bells and whistles to get attention. Second, you don't know a really startling idea when you see one.

When you do use an exclamation point, remember this:

● Use it alone (don't add a comma afterward): "*Holy cow!" said Phil.*

And keep your voice down.

A Brief Interlude:
Parentheses ()

Once in a while you may need an aside, a gentle interruption to tuck information into a sentence or between sentences. One way to enclose this interruption is with parentheses (the end rhymes with *cheese*), and you just now saw a pair.

The thing to know about parentheses is that they can enclose a whole sentence standing alone, or something within a sentence. The tricky part is determining where the other punctuation marks go: inside or outside the closing parenthesis. Punctuation never precedes an opening parenthesis (not in the same sentence, anyway).

- When the aside is a separate sentence, put punctuation inside the parentheses, and start with a capital letter: *Jimmy thinks he has won the lottery. (He is mistaken, however.)*
- When the aside is within a sentence, put punctuation outside the parentheses, and start with a small letter. *Jimmy thinks he has won the lottery (fat chance).*

An exception occurs when the remark inside parentheses is an exclamation (*wow!*) or a question (*huh?*). The exclamation point or question mark goes inside the parentheses, but any accompanying punctuation marks go outside: *Jimmy has already made plans for the money (poor guy!), but his wife is skeptical. He may have misread the numbers on his lottery tickets (how dumb can you get?).*

Too Much of a Good Thing: The Dash (—)

We could do with fewer dashes. In fact, the dash is probably even more overused these days than the exclamation point—and I admit to being an offender myself (there I go again).

The dash is like a detour; it interrupts the sentence and inserts another thought. A single dash can be used in place of a colon to emphatically present some piece of information: *It was what Tina dreaded most—fallen arches.* Or dashes can be used in pairs instead of parentheses to enclose an aside or an explanation: *Her new shoes had loads of style—they were Ferragamos—but not much arch support.*

Dashes thrive in weak writing, because when thoughts are confused, it's easier to stick in a lot of dashes than to organize a smoother sentence. Whenever you are tempted to use dashes, remember this:

● Use no more than two per sentence. And if you do use two, they should act like parentheses to isolate a remark from the rest of the sentence: *After the flight, Tina looked—and she'd be the first to admit it—like an unmade bed.*

- If the gentler and less intrusive parentheses would work as well, use them instead. *Tina's luggage (complete with her return ticket) appeared to be lost.*

By the way, don't confuse the dash with the hyphen (see below). The dash is longer. If you want a dash but your computer keyboard doesn't have one, use two hyphens (--).

Betwixt and Between: The Hyphen (-)

A hyphen is not just a stubby version of the dash. The two of them do very different things. While the dash separates ideas or big chunks in a sentence, the hyphen separates (or connects, depending on how you look at it) individual words or parts of words: *My mother-in-law works for a quasi-official corporation that does two-thirds of its business with the government.*

When a word breaks off at the end of a line in your newspaper and continues on the next line, a hyphen is what links the syllables together. But the hyphen most of us have problems with is the one that goes (or doesn't go) between words, as in terms for some family members (*mother-in-law*), or in two-word descriptions (*quasi-official*), or in fractions (*two-thirds*). Here are some guidelines for when you need a hyphen and when you don't.

The Part-time Hyphen

One of the hardest things to figure out with hyphens is how to use them in two-word descriptions. When two words are combined to describe a noun, sometimes you use a hyphen between them and sometimes you don't.

The first question to ask yourself is whether the description comes before or after the noun.

- If it's after the noun, don't use a hyphen: *Father is strong willed. My cousin is red haired. This chicken is well done.* Ducks are *water resistant*.
- If it's before the noun, use a hyphen when either of the two words in the description wouldn't make very much sense by itself. *He's a strong-willed father. I have a red-haired cousin. This is well-done chicken. Those are water-resistant ducks.*

Exceptional Situations

Here are some exceptions to the "before or after" rule for hyphens in two-word descriptions:

- If *self* or *quasi* is one of the words, always use a hyphen: *Robert is self-effacing; still, he's a self-confident person. He's our quasi-official leader; the position is only quasi-legal.*
- If both words could be used separately and still make sense, don't use a hyphen even if they come before a

noun: *Hodge was a* **naughty old** *cat. Alicia is a* **sweet young** *thing*.

- If *very* is one of the two words, forget the hyphen: *That Hepplewhite is a* **very expensive** *chair*. If *very* is added to a description that would ordinarily take a hyphen (**much-admired** *architect*, for example), drop the hyphen: *Sam's a* **very much admired** *architect*.
- If one of the two words ends in *ly,* you almost never need a hyphen: *That's a* **radically different** *haircut. It gives you an* **entirely new** *look*.
- If one of the words is *most, least,* or *less,* leave out the hyphen: *The* **least likely** *choice, and the* **less costly** *one, is the* **most preposterous** *hat I've ever seen*.

IS YOUR HYPHEN SHOWING?

Here are some cases where you must use hyphens:

- With *ex* (meaning "former"). *Hal is the* **ex-president** *of the company*.
- When adding a beginning or an ending to a word that starts with a capital (*anti-British, Trollope-like*). Two exceptions are *Christlike* and *Antichrist*.
- When adding *like* would create a double or triple *l* (*shell-like*).
- When adding a beginning or ending would create a double vowel (*ultra-average, anti-isolationist*). But *pre* and *re* are often exceptions to this (*preempt, reexamine*),

so when you have a duplicate vowel, look up the word in the dictionary. (The vowels are *a, e, i, o, u.*)

● With fractions. ***Three-quarters** of the brownies and **two-thirds** of the cookies are gone.* For how to go halves, see below.

Half Measures

I wish there were a rule for *half,* but it's all over the map. Some formations involving *half* are one word (*halfhearted, halfway*), some are two words (*half note, half sister*), and some are hyphenated (*half-hour, half-moon*). Check the dictionary.

HEADS OR TAILS

Many of us can't add a beginning or an ending to a word without sticking in a hyphen for good measure. If we put *mini* in front of *van,* it inexplicably becomes *mini-van* instead of *minivan;* if we put *like* after *life,* it unaccountably becomes *life-like,* not *lifelike.* Many hyphens show up where they're not wanted. Here are some common endings and beginnings that don't usually need them:

Endings

ache: I'll trade my **toothache** for your **headache**.

less and *most:* The **ageless** soprano can still hit the **uppermost** notes.

like: What a **lifelike** Gainsborough.

wide: Sewer rats are a **citywide** menace.

Beginnings

anti: Samson was **antifeminist**.

bi: They're conducting a **bicoastal** romance.

co: This celebrity autobiography has no **coauthor**.

extra: His **extracurricular** schedule is full.

inter: Luke has **intergalactic** ambitions.

micro, mini, and *multi:* Excuse me for a moment while I **micromanage** a **minicrisis** among these **multitalented** children.

mid: Our raft sank **midstream**.

non: Hubert is a **nonperson**.

over and *under:* Be **overcautious** if your date is legally **underage**.

post: He lives in a **postwar** building.

pre and *pro:* The **prenuptial** atmosphere was definitely **promarriage**. (See NOTE on page 150.)

re: They have **reexamined** their situation. (See NOTE on page 150.)

semi: I wish I'd invented the **semiconductor**.

sub and *super:* Our **subbasement** got **supersaturated** in the flood.

Hyphens in the Family

Some family members get hyphens and some don't. Here's how to keep them straight.

USE A HYPHEN

- With *ex*. Meet my **ex-husband**.
- With *in-law*. *Fred's my* **brother-in-law**.
- With *great*. *There goes my* **great-aunt**.

DON'T USE A HYPHEN

- With *step*. His **stepson** *Charlie is a doctor.*
- With *half*. *Bob's* **half brother** *is a thug.*
- With *grand*. *She can't be a* **grandmother**!

trans: *Leslie is a **transsexual**.*
ultra: *That Nancy is **ultrachic**.*
un: *Argyle socks with sneakers are **uncool**.*

NOTE: There are exceptions, cases when you'll want to use a hyphen in words starting with *pre*, *pro*, and *re*. If a word starting with *pre* or *pro* is just too hard to read without a hyphen, add one (*pre-iron*, *pro-am*). And if a word starting with *re* could be confused with one that's spelled the same but means something else, add a hyphen. For instance, use *re-cover* (for "cover again") to avoid confusion with the word *recover*. Other examples include *re-creation, re-petition, re-press, re-sent, re-serve, re-sign, re-sort, re-treat.* (When the boss asks to renew your employment contract, it makes a big difference whether your reply memo says, "I'm going to re-sign" or "I'm going to resign.")

A Multitalented Mark: The Apostrophe (')

That little airborne mark that dangles over some words (including last names like O'Conner) is called an apostrophe. This is the punctuation mark that has many sign painters mystified. Store awnings and windows, sides of trucks, even neon signs, are peppered with wayward apostrophes that either don't belong at all or are in the wrong position. Beware, especially, of the unusual apostrophe in a plural word.

Here's how to use an apostrophe with . . .

• **Possessives.** To indicate ownership, add *'s* to a singular noun or to a plural noun that does not end in *s*: **Buster's** *bulldog has wrecked the* **children's** *room.* Add the apostrophe alone to a plural noun that ends in *s*:

This was the boys' idea. (Chapter 3 is all about possessives, in case you need to know more.)

- **Some unusual plurals.** Add *'s* to make plurals of numbers and letters, including abbreviations: *Libby, the daughter of two CPA's, was born in the 1940's, and earned all B's at Swarthmore.* When a number is written out, it gets no apostrophe: *She spent **millions** of dollars in **tens** and **twenties**.* For more on the sticky question of using apostrophes to make plurals, see page 30.

- **Missing letters.** An apostrophe can show where letters have been dropped in a shortened word or phrase. For example, *shouldn't* is short for *should not;* the apostrophe shows where the *o* in *not* was dropped. Some other clipped words are quite irregular, like *won't* and the illegitimate *ain't.* Shortened words and phrases are called contractions; there's a list of them on pages 73–74 (they're also in the dictionary). When in doubt, look it up.

- **A comma or period.** When you need a comma or period (or any other punctuation, for that matter) after a possessive word that ends with an apostrophe, the punctuation goes after the apostrophe: *The idea was the boys', but the responsibility was their **parents**'.*

Enough Said:
Quotation Marks (" ")

Think of quotation marks as bookends that support a quotation in between.

The opening quotation marks always go right before the first word of the quotation: *"Can we talk?"* The trick is at the other end, where the closing quotation marks go. You'll have to decide whether the punctuation that follows the quoted material (period, comma, question mark, or whatever) goes inside or outside the closing quotation marks. Here's what's in and what's out.

The Ins

- **Period.** *"I think I'm going to be sick."*
- **Comma.** *"I shouldn't have eaten those strawberries,"* Gustav said.

The Outs

- **Colon.** *There are two reasons she hates the nickname "Honey": It's sticky and it's sweet.*
- **Semicolon.** *Frank's favorite song was "My Way"; he recorded it several times.*

Sometimes In,
Sometimes Out

- **Question mark.** In most cases, a question mark should be inside the quotation marks: *"Who goes there?"* said the sentry. *"What is the password?"* But the question mark must be outside if it's not part of the actual quotation: *Who starred in "Dynasty"?*

- **Exclamation point.** In most cases, an exclamation point goes inside the quotation marks: *"Captain!" said Sulu. "We're losing speed!"* But the exclamation point goes outside if it's not part of the quotation: *My God, the screen just went blank after reading "Situation Normal"!*

- **Parentheses.** If the entire quotation is in parentheses, then the closing parenthesis should go outside the quotation marks: *Uhura had the last word ("I told you so").* If only part of the quotation is in parentheses, then the closing parenthesis goes inside the quotation marks: *She added, "Maybe next time you'll listen to me (if there is a next time)."*

- **Apostrophe.** How do we get ourselves into messes like this one? To create the possessive of something that's normally in quotation marks—for example, the title of a poem, "The Raven"—you would have to put the apostrophe outside: *"The Raven"'s first stanza is the best.* Pretty awful-looking, isn't it? It's so awful that many publications even cheat to avoid it, and write *"The Raven's"*—definitely incorrect, although much prettier. My advice is to avoid this problem entirely. Instead of writing *"The Raven"'s author was Poe,* rearrange it: *Poe was the author of "The Raven."*

NOTE: When one quotation appears within another, enclose the interior one in single quotation marks: *"Was it Linus who said, 'Get lost'?" asked Lucy.*

The Slant on Titles

You may have wondered why some titles, like *Vogue* and *Huckleberry Finn,* most often appear in the slanting letters called italics, while others, like "Bedroom at Arles" and "My Funny Valentine," usually appear in ordinary type enclosed in quotation marks.

Customs vary on how titles should be written. In most newspaper writing, for example, all titles are in plain type, though not all go inside quotation marks.

My advice is to follow conventional practice. Put the names of larger works, like books, movies, and plays (and magazines and newspapers), in italics. Put the names of smaller works, like poems, stories, and paintings, in ordinary type with quotation marks.

Use Italics

Books: *Gone With the Wind*
Magazines: *Newsweek*
Newspapers: *The Miami Herald*
Movies: *Million Dollar Legs*

The Less Said:
When Not to Quote

Sign painters seem to love quotation marks. They don't care how a word is spelled, as long as it's enclosed in quotes. I don't know much about the sign-painting business—maybe they get paid extra for punctuation. Here are a few signs of the times I've spotted:

Nail salon: *Our Instruments Are "Sterilized"*
Pizzeria: *"Free" Delivery*
Locksmith: *"Fast" and "Friendly" Service*

There's no reason for quotation marks in any of those signs. The intent may be to emphasize the quoted words, but a bright color or a different typeface would do a better job.

In fact, quotation marks used like that can mislead the reader. They're sometimes used in a skeptical or sarcastic way, to indicate that what's quoted isn't meant seriously: *Uncle Oscar's regular Friday-night "volunteer work" turned out to be a poker game.*

The moral is: Don't quote it if you don't have to. And the next time your pipes spring a leak and a truck marked *"Licensed" Plumber* pulls up to your door, don't say I didn't warn you.

Plays, musicals, operas, ballets: *Macbeth, Guys and Dolls, The Magic Flute, Swan Lake*

Use Quotation Marks

Articles: "The Cellulite Cure: Fact or Fiction?"

Essays: "Civil Disobedience," by Henry David Thoreau

Poems: "The Raven," by Edgar Allan Poe

Short stories: "The Secret Life of Walter Mitty," by James Thurber

Paintings, sculptures: "Nude Descending a Staircase," "Venus de Milo"

TV series: "Jeopardy!"

Song titles: "Begin the Beguine"

NOTE: Where titles are concerned, classical music has its own variations on the theme. Here, too, usage varies widely. I recommend writing the formal names of symphonies, concertos, sonatas, and similar compositions in ordinary type without quotation marks: Mahler's Symphony No. 2 in C Minor, Mozart's Serenade in D. But if you use a nickname, put it in quotation marks: Beethoven's "Emperor" Concerto, Schubert's "Trout" Quintet.

Chapter 7

The Compleat Dangler

A Fish out of Water

Life would be pretty dull if everyone's English were perfect. Without slips of the tongue, we wouldn't have spoonerisms, the tongue-tanglers named after the befuddled Reverend William A. Spooner. He was the Victorian clergyman who spoke of "Kinquering Congs" and greeted someone with, "I remember your name perfectly, but I just can't think of your face."

And we wouldn't have malapropisms, either. Mrs. Malaprop was a character in an eighteenth-century play whose bungled attempts at erudite speech led her to declare one gentleman "the very pineapple of politeness!" and to say of another, "Illiterate him . . . from your memory."

We're lucky that English, with its stretchy grammar and its giant grab-bag of a vocabulary, gives us so much room for verbal play, if not anarchy. As Groucho Marx said, "Love flies out the door when money comes innuendo," and it's hard to imagine him saying it in Esperanto.

Naturally, if you have room to play, you have room to make mistakes. And English sentences are often constructed without regard for building codes. I've grown almost fond of one common error, the dangler. It's a word or phrase (a group of words) that's in the wrong place at the wrong time, so it ends up describing the wrong thing. Here comes one now: *Strolling along the trail, Mount Rushmore came into view.* The opening phrase, *strolling along the trail,* is a dangler. Why? Because it's attached to the wrong thing, *Mount Rushmore.* The way the sentence stands, the mountain was out taking a stroll!

Danglers show up in newspapers and bestsellers, on the network news and highway billboards, and they can be endlessly entertaining—as long as they're perpetrated by someone else. When you're doing the talking or writing, the scrambled sentence isn't so amusing. See if you can tell what's wrong with these examples.

● *Born at the age of forty-three, the baby was a great comfort to Mrs. Wooster.* As the sentence is arranged, the baby—not his mother—was forty-three. (The opening phrase, *born at the age of forty-three,* is attached to *the baby,* so that's what it describes.) Here's one way to re-arrange things: *The baby, born when Mrs. Wooster was forty-three, was a great comfort to her.*

- *Tail wagging merrily, Bertie took the dog for a walk.* See how *tail wagging merrily* is attached to *Bertie*? Put the tail on the dog: *Tail wagging merrily, the dog went for a walk with Bertie.*
- *As a den mother, Mrs. Glossop's station wagon was always full of Cub Scouts.* Whoa! The phrase *as a den mother* is attached to *Mrs. Glossop's station wagon*. Attach it to the lady herself: *As a den mother, Mrs. Glossop always had her station wagon full of Cub Scouts.*

Danglers are like mushrooms in the woods—they're hard to see at first, but once you get the hang of it they're easy to find. Although the wild dangler may lurk almost anywhere in a sentence, the seasoned hunter will look in the most obvious place, right at the beginning of the sentence. If the first phrase is hitched to the wrong wagon—or no wagon at all—it's a dangler. Some kinds of opening phrases are more likely than others to be out of place. I'll show you what to look for.

THE USUAL SUSPECT

Always suspect an *ing* word of dangling if it's near the front of a sentence; consider it guilty until proved innocent. To find the culprit, ask yourself whodunit. Who's doing the *walking, talking, singing,* or whatever? You may be surprised by the answer. In these examples, look at the phrase containing the *ing* word and look at whodunit.

- *After overeating, the hammock looked pretty good to Archie.* Who ate too much in this sentence? The hammock! If a person did the overeating, the opening *ing* phrase should be attached to him: *After overeating,* **Archie** *thought the hammock looked pretty good.*

- *On returning home, Maxine's phone rang.* Who came home? Maxine's phone! To show that the owner of the phone was doing the returning, put her right after the opening phrase: *On returning home,* **Maxine** *heard the phone ring.*

- *Walking briskly, the belt of her raincoat was lost.* Who's the pedestrian? The belt! What's attached to the opening phrase is what's doing the walking. If you want to say *she* was walking briskly, put her right after the opening phrase: *Walking briskly,* **she** *lost the belt of her raincoat.*

PIN THE TAIL ON THE DONKEY

Have you ever seen children at parties pinning the tail on the wrong part of the donkey? Well, sometimes adjectives (words that characterize nouns) get pinned to the wrong part of a sentence and become danglers. Here's a sentence with its "tail" in the wrong place:

Incorrect: **Dumpy and overweight,** *the vet says our dog needs more exercise.*

The description *dumpy and overweight* should be pinned on the dog, not the vet:

Correct: **Dumpy and overweight**, *our dog needs more exercise, the vet says*. A more graceful solution would be to rewrite the sentence completely: *The vet says our dog needs more exercise because she's* **dumpy and overweight**.

Adjectives (such as *dumpy* and *overweight*) like to be pinned on the nearest noun.

HITCH YOUR WAGON

A dangling adverb at the front of a sentence is a lot like a horse that's hitched to the wrong wagon. Adverbs (words that characterize verbs) can be easy to spot because they often end in *ly*. When you see one, make sure it's "hitched" to the right verb. In this example, what went wrong at the hitching post?

Incorrect: **Miraculously** *we watched as the surgeon operated with a plastic spoon*.

As the sentence stands, the opening word, *miraculously*, refers to the watching, not the operating. That's because the closest verb is *watched*. To fix things, put the *ly* word closer to the right action:

Correct: **Miraculously**, *the surgeon operated with a plastic spoon as we watched*.

Here's another solution: *We watched as the surgeon* **miraculously** *operated with a plastic spoon*.

Adverbs (such as *miraculously*) like to be hitched to the nearest verb. For another warning about troublesome adverbs, see page 130.

ROADS TO NOWHERE

You can easily be led astray when a sentence has a road sign at the very beginning. The kind of sign I mean is a preposition, a word that shows position or direction (*at, by, on, with,* and so on). If the sign is in the wrong place, you end up on the road to nowhere. Try to avoid this kind of dangler:

Incorrect: **At the age of ten**, *my father bought me a puppy.*

As the sentence is written, Dad was only a boy! That's because the opening phrase, *at the age of ten,* is attached to *my father*—an obvious mismatch. If the sign is to point in the right direction, the sentence has to be rearranged:

Correct: **At the age of ten**, *I got a puppy from my father.*

Or: *My father bought me a puppy* **when I was ten.**

TO'S A CROWD

Some of the hardest danglers to see begin with *to.* Beware of the sentence that starts with an infinitive (a verb form usually preceded by *to,* for instance *to run, to see, to build*). The opening phrase has to be attached to whoever or whatever is performing the action. Here's an opening phrase that leaves the sentence scrambled:

Incorrect: **To crack an egg properly**, *the yolk is left intact.*

As the sentence is written, the yolk is the one cracking the egg. The opening phrase, *to crack an egg properly,* is attached to *the yolk,* not to whoever is doing the cracking. Let's put a cook in the kitchen.

Exceptions That Make the Rule

Some expressions are so common that they're allowed to dangle at the beginning of a sentence, even though they're not connected to anything in particular. We treat them as casually as throat-clearing. For example, we may say: **Generally speaking**, *pigeons mate for life.* The pigeons aren't the ones doing the speaking, naturally, and no one would make such a connection. Other stock phrases that can dangle to their hearts' content include *strictly speaking, barring unforeseen circumstances, considering the alternative, assuming the worst, judging by appearances, after all, by and large, on the whole, admittedly, put simply, given the conditions, in the long run, in the final analysis, to tell the truth, contrary to popular belief,* and *to be perfectly frank.* Introductory phrases like these have become so familiar that they have earned the right to be exceptions to the rule. Are they necessary? That's another issue. For more about throat-clearing, see page 197.

Correct: *To crack an egg properly, you must leave the yolk intact.*

Here's an even simpler way to say it: *To crack an egg properly, leave the yolk intact.* (The subject is understood to be *you*. This is called an imperative sentence, since someone's being told to do something.)

Owners' manuals, you'll notice, are chock-full of dangling infinitives. Does this sound familiar? *To activate widget A, doohickey B is inserted into slot C.* If the one trying to activate the silly thing is *you*, make *you* the subject: *To activate widget A, you insert doohickey B into slot C.* Or you can delete the *you*, since it's understood to be the subject: *To activate widget A, insert doohickey B into slot C.*

A LIKELY STORY

Looking for a dangler? Then look for a sentence that starts with *like* or *unlike*. More than likely, you'll find a boo-boo. Here's a likely candidate.

Incorrect: *Like Alice, Fran's nose job cost plenty.*

The phrase *like Alice* is a dangler because it's attached to the wrong thing: *Fran's nose job.* Presumably Fran, and not her nose job, is *like* Alice. Make sure the things being compared really are comparable. There are two ways to fix a sentence like this.

Correct: *Like Alice, Fran paid plenty for her nose job.* Or: *Like Alice's, Fran's nose job cost plenty.*

Chapter 8

Death Sentence

Do Clichés Deserve to Die?

Tallulah Bankhead once described herself as "pure as the driven slush." And bankruptcy has been called "a fate worse than debt." We smile at expressions like these out of relief, because we're braced for the numbing cliché that fails to arrive.

Nothing is wrong with using a figure of speech, an expression that employs words in imaginative (or "figurative") ways to throw in a little vividness or surprise. But it's an irony of human communication that the more beautiful or lively or effective the figure of speech, the more likely it will be loved, remembered, repeated, worn out, and finally worked to death. That's why some people will tell you that the Bible and Shakespeare are full of clichés!

So crowded is our stock of figurative language that every

profession—legal, corporate, fashion, artistic, literary, and so on—seems to have a collection all its own. A tired book critic, for example, will say a novel is "a richly woven tapestry," "a tour de force," or "a cautionary tale," one whose characters are either "coming of age" or experiencing "rites of passage." For corporate "high rollers," what matters is the "bottom line," or whether a company is "in play," or a stock has "gone south."

Then are all clichés and familiar turns of phrase to be summarily executed? No. Let your ear be your guide. If a phrase sounds expressive and lively and nothing else will do, fine. If it sounds flat, be merciless. One more point. It's far better to trot out a dependable cliché, and to use it as is, than to deck it out with lame variations (*the tip of the proverbial iceberg*) or to get it wrong ("unchartered seas" instead of *uncharted* ones; "high dungeon" instead of *dudgeon;* "heart-rendering" instead of *heart-rending*). And two unrelated figures of speech shouldn't be used one after the other, whether they're clichés or not (*He got off his high horse and went back to the drawing board*). That's called mixing your metaphors, and there's more about it at the end of this chapter.

There's no way to eliminate all clichés. It would take a roomful of Shakespeares to replace them with fresh figures of speech, and before long those would become clichés, too. Vivid language is recycled precisely because it's vivid. But think of clichés as condiments, the familiar ketchup, mustard, and relish of language. Use when appropriate, and don't use too much. When you're dressing up a hamburger, you don't use béarnaise sauce. You use ketchup, and that's as it should be. But you don't put it on everything. Some dishes, after all, call for something special. Here are some of today's more overworked condiments.

Acid test. Overuse and you flunk.

Agree to disagree. People never really *agree to disagree.* They just get tired of arguing.

Back to the drawing board. Back to *Roget's Thesaurus.*

The ball is in your court. Only if you're Andre Agassi.

Beat a dead horse. Anyone who uses this expression more than once a month should be required to send a donation to the ASPCA.

Bite the bullet. Save your teeth.

Bitter end. This is right up there with *making ends meet.*

Blanket of snow. Nature is a *fertile field* (there's another one) for clichés. Besides *blankets of snow,* beware *sheets of rain, calms before the storm, devastating earthquakes, raging torrents, bolts from the blue, steaming jungles, uncharted seas* (which are likely to become *watery graves*), *wide-open spaces, places in the sun,* and anything *silhouetted against the sky.* (See also *golf-ball-sized hail* below.)

Blessing in disguise. Not disguised well enough.

Boggles the mind. It's all right to be boggled once in a while, but don't make a habit of it.

Bone of contention. This expression is getting osteoporosis.

Bored to tears. There has to be a more exciting way to complain of boredom.

Bottom line. Unless—and even if—you're talking about finance, there's probably a better way to say it.

Broad daylight. The sun has begun to set on this one, and on *light of day.*

Brute force. This phrase is no longer forceful.

A bug going around. Another way of saying you don't know what you've got.

By hook or by crook. This one hangs out in the same crowd with *hook, line, and sinker* and *lock, stock, and barrel.*

Can of worms. Don't open this one too often. And don't unnecessarily disturb its cousins, *nest of vipers* and *hornet's nest.*

Can't see the forest for the trees. If you find yourself using this expression over and over again, you have a myopic imagination.

Champing at the bit. If you must use it, get it straight. Restless horses *champ* at their bits; they don't "chomp."

Come to a head. Sometimes seen as *bring to a head*, this phrase has its humble beginnings in dermatology. Need I say more?

Cool as a cucumber. Using this too much is uncool.

Cutting edge. Dull.

Days are numbered. A phrase that's not just overused, but depressing.

Dead as a doornail. Why a doornail, anyway? (Also see *passed away* below).

Diamond in the rough. And watch those *pearls before swine*, too. When accessorizing your language, remember that a little jewelry goes a long way.

Discreet silence. Silence makes good clichés (*chilly silence, eloquent silence*). And in the silence, of course, you can *hear a pin drop*.

Draw a blank. This is what you do when you run out of clichés.

Each and every. The resort of a weak writer, like *one and the same* and *any and all*.

Easier said than done. What isn't? As for *no sooner said than done*, it's a promise that's seldom kept.

Errand of mercy. The truly merciful don't resort to clichés.

Far be it from me. When you say this, you're about to butt in where you don't belong. If you do want to be a buttinsky, though, use it correctly (not "far be it for me").

Fell through the cracks. An unconvincing way of saying something is not your fault. And don't make it worse by saying "fell between the cracks."

Few and far between. This is what fresh expressions are becoming.

Food for thought. I'd say this expression is *from hunger,* but that's another cliché.

Fools rush in. And when they get there, they use clichés.

Foregone conclusion. A pedestrian way of saying that something was no surprise.

Foreseeable future. The future is not foreseeable. Anyone who knows otherwise should be in the commodities market.

General consensus. Disagreeable.

Generation gap. An even worse cliché, *Generation X,* is already geriatric.

Get nowhere fast. It's a cliché, all right, but it's better than *spinning your wheels.*

Get the show on the road. This expression closed in New Haven.

Glass ceiling. This phrase, like *level playing field,* is getting overworked. Hasn't it become a little transparent?

Golf-ball-sized hail. Why golf balls? How about plums or Ping-Pong balls for a change?

Grind to a halt. OK, you can use this maybe once a year.

Head over heels. I've never understood this one. Wouldn't *heels over head* make more sense?

Heated argument. Is there any other kind?

His own worst enemy. Not unless he stabs himself in the back.

Impenetrable fog. Maybe we should bring back *thick as pea soup.*

In the nick of time. "Just in time" isn't good enough?

Innocent bystander. Why is a *bystander* always *innocent*? Has anybody given him a lie-detector test?

It goes without saying. Then don't say it.

Last but not least. If it's not least, then don't put it last.

Leaps and bounds. Gazelles and antelopes, and maybe even lizards, move by *leaps and bounds;* few other things do.

Legendary. This and *fabled* are much overused. What legend? What fable? Unless you're Aesop or the Brothers Grimm, give these words a vacation.

Make a killing. The best thing to be said about this cliché is that it's better than being *taken to the cleaners.* Don't use either of them to excess.

Mass exodus. As opposed to an exodus of one? In most cases, *exodus* alone is enough.

Meaningful dialogue. This was a dumb expression to begin with. Drop *meaningful.* In fact, *dialogue* is pretty dumb, too. Don't people have talks anymore?

Moment of truth. Ever notice that it's always bad news?

More than meets the eye. If you've got a good eye, there's not that much more.

Nip it in the bud. This nipping of buds has to stop.

Pandora's box. Put a lid on it.

Passed away. You've probably noticed that death is a favorite playground of clichés. This is too bad. In situations where people most need sincerity, what do they get? Denial. There's no shame in saying somebody died, but the vocabulary of mortality avoids it. Think again before using expressions like *passed away* or *passed on* (sometimes reduced to just *passed*), *untimely end, cut down in his prime, called to his Maker, called away, great beyond, this mortal coil, bought the farm, hopped the twig* (a variation on *fell off his perch*), *kicked the bucket, gone to a better place, handed in his dinner pail, checked out, grim reaper, in the midst of life, irreparable loss, broke the mold, vale of tears, time heals all, words can't express, tower of strength,* or *he looks like he's sleeping.*

Play hardball. This expression seems to have edged out *no more Mr. Nice Guy.* But it's not as intimidating as it once was, so why not give it a rest?

Play it by ear. This is a nice old image. Let's not wear it out, except at the piano.

Political hopefuls. I vote no.

Powers that be. This is much overused by powers that wannabe.

Pre-existing condition. We're probably stuck with this, but it's a redundancy (that means it repeats itself, like *end result, final outcome, new initiative,* and *close proximity*).

Pushing the envelope. Isn't it amazing how fast a new phrase gets old? Like *A-OK,* this one is no longer state-of-the-art.

Raise the bar. May it go belly-up.

Reliable source. Are your other sources lying scoundrels?

Roller coaster. This phrase (usually preceded by some descriptive term like *emotional* or *fiscal*) comes up a lot in news stories about natural disasters, crippling illness, the federal budget, or the Olympic Games. Let's hope the ride will soon be over.

Sadder but wiser. Some people are *sadder but wiser* after hearing *a word to the wise.* These are nice old expressions that could be with us for a long time if they're treated gently, but *only time will tell*.

Sea of faces. These are often *bright and shining faces*. Commencement speakers, why not give these expressions a sabbatical?

Seat of the pants. And very shiny pants they are. Let's not wear them out.

Seriously consider. This isn't just hackneyed, it's insincere. If someone tells you he'll *seriously consider* your suggestion, he's already kissed it off. That goes double if he has promised to give it *active* or *due consideration*.

Shattered with grief. Why does this phrase make us think of insincere widows?

Sickening thud. This was a lively image in the first five thousand mystery novels where it appeared. The *sickening thud* usually came after *a shot rang out*.

Slippery slope. Don't fall for it.

Tarnished image. The *tarnished image* (distantly related to the old *blot on the escutcheon*) could use some polishing. Give it a leave of absence.

Team player. When your boss says you should be more of a *team player*, that means she wants you to take on more of her work.

Thick as thieves. Thieves are not that thick, anyway. Otherwise, plea bargaining would never work.

Tip of the iceberg. A tip of the hat to anyone who can come up with something better.

To the manner born. If you're going to use a cliché, respect it. This Shakespearean phrase (it comes from *Hamlet*) means "accustomed to" or "familiar with" a manner of living. It is not "to the manor born" and has nothing to do with manor houses.

Tongue in cheek. The only expression more trite than *tongue in cheek* is *tongue firmly in cheek.* I'd like to retire them both.

Trust implicitly. Never believe anybody who says you can trust him implicitly.

Tumultuous applause. This went out with the Monkees.

24/7. Time out!

Up in the air. Let's come up with a more down-to-earth way of saying this.

Viable alternative. Well, it beats the alternative that doesn't work.

War-torn. This cliché stays alive because, regrettably, there are always enough wars to go around. Anything that's *war-torn,* by the way, is bound to be *embattled* or *besieged.*

What makes him tick. This image is winding down. Don't overdo it.

World-class. No class.

Metaphors Be with You

Is it any wonder we love figures of speech? Just think how dull language would be without them. The metaphor, the most common figure of speech, lets us use one image—any image we want!—to conjure up another. Imagination is the only limit. This gives us about a zillion ways (give or take a few) of saying the same thing.

The phrase *volley of abuse,* for example, uses the image of a fusillade of bullets to describe an outpouring of anger. This metaphor leaves behind a single vivid picture.

But if that image has to compete with another (as in, *The volley of abuse was the straw that broke the camel's back*), we have what's called a mixed metaphor. No clear picture emerges, just two dueling ideas (bullets versus straws). If you've heard it's unwise to mix metaphors, this is why: The competing images drown each other out, as in, *the silver lining at the end of the tunnel,* or *Don't count your chickens till the cows come home.*

Some people are so wild about metaphors that they can't resist using them in pairs. This may work, if the images don't clash: *Frieda viewed her marriage as a tight ship, but Lorenzo was plotting a mutiny.* Since the images of *tight ship* and *mutiny* have an idea in common (sailing), they blend into one picture. But usually when two figures of speech appear together, they aren't so compatible. In that case, the less said, the better.

Chapter 9

The Living Dead

Let Bygone Rules Be Gone

The house of grammar has many rooms, and some of them are haunted. Despite the best efforts of grammatical exorcists, the ghosts of dead rules and the spirits of imaginary taboos are still rattling and thumping about the old place.

Sometimes an ancient prohibition becomes outdated, or it may turn out that a musty convention was never really a rule at all. The trouble is that these phantoms are hard to displace, once they take hold in our minds. It's no longer considered a crime to split an infinitive or end a sentence with a preposition, for example, but the specters of bogus or worn-out rules have a way of coming back to haunt us. In the interest of laying a few to rest, I dedicate to each a tombstone, complete with burial service. May they rest in peace.

TOMBSTONE: Don't split an infinitive.

R.I.P. An infinitive is a verb in its simplest form, right out of the box. It can usually be recognized by the word *to* in front of it: *Blackbeard helped him to escape*. But the *to* isn't actually part of the infinitive and isn't always necessary: *Blackbeard helped him escape*. As a preposition, a word that positions other words, the *to* lets us know an infinitive is coming.

The truth is that the phrase "split infinitive" is misleading. Since *to* isn't really part of the infinitive, there's nothing to split. A sentence often sounds better when the *to* is close to the infinitive: *Dilbert decided **to mention** dating in the workplace*. But there's no harm in separating them by putting a descriptive word or two in between: *Dilbert decided **to discreetly mention** dating in the workplace*.

A sentence like that sounds natural because in English, the best place for an adverb (like *discreetly*) is right in front of the word it describes (*mention*). Where else could *discreetly* go? Putting it anywhere else—say, before or after *decided* or *dating*—would change the meaning. So go ahead and split, but don't overdo it. Not: *Dilbert decided **to discreetly and without referring to the boss's secretary mention** dating in the workplace*.

Sometimes, rearranging a sentence to avoid a "split" makes it ridiculous. Try this example: *Kiri's landlord wanted **to flatly forbid** singing*. Or this one: *He threatened **to more than double** her rent*. Or this: *The landlord is expected **to strongly oppose** weaker noise regulations*. See what I mean?

Writers of English have been merrily "splitting" infinitives since the 1300's. It was considered perfectly acceptable until the mid-nineteenth century, when Latin scholars—notably Henry Alford in his book *A Plea for the Queen's English*—misguidedly called it a crime. (Some linguists trace the taboo to the Victorians' slavish fondness for Latin, a language in which you *can't* divide an infinitive.) This "rule" was popular for half a century, until leading grammarians debunked it. But its ghost has proved more durable than Freddy Krueger.

TOMBSTONE: It's wrong to end a sentence with a preposition.

R.I.P. Here's another bugaboo that English teachers used to get worked up over.

We can blame an eighteenth-century English clergyman and Latin scholar named Robert Lowth for popularizing this one. He wrote the first grammar book to say that a preposition (a positioning word, like *at, by, for, into, off, on, out, over, to, under, up, with*) shouldn't go at the end of a sentence. This idea caught on, even though great literature from Chaucer to Shakespeare to Milton is bristling with sentences ending in prepositions. Nobody knows why the notion stuck—possibly because it's closer to Latin grammar, or perhaps because the word *preposition* means "position before," which seems to suggest that a preposition can't come last.

At any rate, this is a rule that modern grammarians have long tried to get us out from under.

🪦 **TOMBSTONE:** *Data* is a plural noun and always takes a plural verb.

R.I.P. It's time to admit that *data* has joined *agenda, erotica, insignia, opera,* and other technically plural Latin and Greek words that have become thoroughly Anglicized as singular nouns taking singular verbs. No plural form is necessary, and the old singular form, *datum,* can be left to the Romans. (*Media,* it seems, is going the same way, though it's not there yet. Ask me again in a few years.)

🪦 **TOMBSTONE:** Always put the subject of a sentence before the verb.

R.I.P. Says who? Tell it to Tennyson (*"Into the valley of Death / Rode the six hundred"*). He didn't mind putting his subject (*the six hundred*) after the verb (*rode*).

True, most of the time a sentence with its subject (the one doing the action) before the verb (the action being done) sounds more forceful and direct than one written the other way around. *Murray came later* has more oomph than *Later came Murray.* But every now and then it's appropriate to put the verb first (*Says who?* for instance), and literature is full of poetic examples of verbs preceding their subjects. (Just ask Poe: *"Quoth the Raven, 'Nevermore.'"*)

NOTE: If a sentence starts with *there,* its real subject probably follows the verb, as in: *There was a young*

man from Darjeeling. (The subject isn't *there*; it's *man.*)
Sentences starting with *there* get a bad rap in many
grammar guides. There's nothing wrong with them, either. See pages 55 and 192.

TOMBSTONE: It's wrong to start a sentence with *and*
or *but*.

R.I.P. But why is it wrong? There's no law against
occasionally using *and* or *but* to begin a sentence.

Over the years, some English teachers have enforced the
notion that *and* and *but* should be used only to join elements
within a sentence, not to join one sentence with another. Not
so. It's been common practice to begin sentences with them
since at least as far back as the tenth century. But don't
overdo it, or your writing will sound monotonous.

TOMBSTONE: Don't split the parts of a verb phrase
(like *has been*).

R.I.P. This has never been a rule. It's a by-product of
the famous superstition about splitting an infinitive (see the
first tombstone, page 182).

TOMBSTONE: *None* is always singular.

R.I.P. Not always. In fact, *none* is more likely to be
plural.

Many people seem to have been taught (mistakenly) that
none always means "not one" (as in, **None of the chickens is**

hatched). But most authorities have always believed that *none* is closer in meaning to "not any (of them)" than to "not one (of them)." So it's considered plural in most cases and takes a plural verb: **None** of the chickens **are** hatched.

None is singular only when it means "none of it"—that is to say, "no amount." (**None** of the milk **was** spilled.)

If you really do mean "not one," say "not one." (There's more about *none* in the chapter on plurals, page 27.)

TOMBSTONE: Don't use *whose* to refer to inanimate objects.

R.I.P. Here's a musty old custom whose time is up. There's nothing wrong with using the possessive *whose* for inanimate objects. *Never buy a **car whose** odometer doesn't work.*

A related misconception is that you shouldn't use *'s* with inanimate things (as in *This **car's** odometer is broken*). Apparently, the thinking goes, inanimate things aren't as possessive as living ones. Silly, right? Well this book's position is that yesterday's custom can be safely ignored.

TOMBSTONE: Use *It is I*, not *It is me*.

R.I.P. Here's another ordinance that's out-of-date. In all but the most formal circumstances, it's OK to use *It is me, That's him, It's her,* and similar constructions, instead of the technically correct but stuffier *It is I, That's he,* and *It's she.*

Similarly, it's fine to say *Me too.* The alternative, *I too,* is still grammatically correct, but unless you're addressing the Supreme Court or the Philological Society, you can drop the formality.

There's more about *I* and *me* on pages 10–12.

TOMBSTONE: Never use *who* when the rules call for *whom*.

R.I.P. We can't dump *whom* entirely, at least not just yet. But many modern grammarians believe that in conversation or informal writing, *who* is acceptable in place of *whom* at the beginning of a sentence or clause (a clause is a group of words with its own subject and verb): **Who's the package for?** *You'll never guess **who** I ran into the other day.*

Where *whom* should be used after a preposition (*to, from, behind, on,* etc.), you can substitute *who* in casual situations by reversing the order and putting *who* in front. *"From **whom**?"* becomes *"**Who** from?"*

There's a more detailed discussion of *who* versus *whom* on pages 6–10.

TOMBSTONE: Always use an active verb (*Bonnie **drove** the getaway car*) and avoid a passive one (*The getaway car **was driven** by Bonnie*).

R.I.P. It's true that a passive verb makes for a wimpier, more roundabout way of saying something. The more straightforward way is to put the one performing the action (*Bonnie*) ahead of the one being acted upon (*the getaway car*), with the verb in between: subject . . . verb . . . object.

But the direct way isn't always the best way. The passive might be more appropriate in cases like these:

- When there's a punch line. You might want to place the one performing the action at the end of the sentence for emphasis or surprise: *The gold medal in the five-hundred-meter one-man bobsled competition **has been won** by a six-year-old child!*
- When nobody cares whodunit. Sometimes the one performing the action isn't even mentioned: *Hermione **has been arrested**. Witherspoon **is being treated** for a gunshot wound.* We don't need to know who put the cuffs on Hermione, or who's stitching up Witherspoon.

TOMBSTONE: Never use a double negative.

R.I.P. My advice on double negatives: Never say never.

The double negative wasn't always a no-no. For centuries, it was fine to pile one negative on top of another in the same sentence. Chaucer and Shakespeare did this all the time to accentuate the negative. It wasn't until the eighteenth century that the double negative was declared a sin against the King's English, on the ground that one negative canceled the other. (Blame Robert Lowth, the same guy who decided we shouldn't put a preposition at the end of a sentence.)

As for now, stay away from the most flagrant examples (*I*

didn't do nothing; You never take me nowhere), but don't write off the double negative completely. It's handy when you want to avoid coming right out and saying something: *Your blind date is not unattractive. I wouldn't say I don't like your new haircut.* (There's more on double negatives in the glossary.)

TOMBSTONE: Use *I shall* instead of *I will.*

R.I.P. Once upon a time, refined folk always used *I shall* or *we shall* to refer to the simple future, not *I will* or *we will.* But *will* has edged out *shall* as the people's choice. *Shall* can still be used with *I* and *we* in an offer or a proposal: **Shall I** *freshen your drink, or* **shall we** *go?*

There's more about the demise of *shall* in the chapter on verbs (page 71).

TOMBSTONE: Use *more than* instead of *over.*

R.I.P. You may have been told by some pedant that *over* doesn't apply to numbers, only to quantities. Not so. It's fine to use *over* in place of *more than* or *in excess of*: *Dad's new car gets* **over** *ten miles to the gallon.*

TOMBSTONE: Don't use *since* to mean "because."

R.I.P. Now and then, an extremely conservative grammarian will suggest that *since* should be used only to indicate a time period (*since Thursday,* for example). Forget that, if you ever heard it. *Since* doesn't always mean "from the time that."

It can also mean "because" or "for the reason that." (*Since you asked me, I'll tell you.*) People have been using *since* in this way for five hundred years.

Just be sure the meaning can't be confused, as in, **Since we spoke, I've had second thoughts.** In that case, *since* could mean either "from the time that" or "because," so it's better to be more precise.

TOMBSTONE: Don't use *while* to mean "although."

R.I.P. Some grammarians believe that *while,* which comes from an Anglo-Saxon word meaning "time," should be used only to mean "during the time that."

But there's a long tradition, going back at least to the sixteenth century, of using *while* at the head of a sentence to mean "although" or "whereas": **While** *he may be short, he's wiry.*

Just be sure the meaning can't be confused, as in: **While** *he reads the* Times, *he watches the news on CNN.* In this case, *while* could mean either "during the time that" or "although." Pick one of those and avoid the confusion.

One more thing about *while.* Some people overuse it as a way to vary their sentences and avoid using *and.* Let's not wear out a useful word for no good reason. If *while* isn't meant, don't use it. Not: *Wally wears suspenders,* **while** *his favorite shoes are wingtips.*

TOMBSTONE: Use *lighted,* not *lit.*

R.I.P. There's nothing wrong with using *lit* for the past tense of *light: Paul **lit** two cigarettes, then gave one to Bette.*

TOMBSTONE: Use *have got,* not *have gotten.*

R.I.P. People who take this prohibition seriously have gotten their grammar wrong.

At one time, everyone agreed that the verb *get* had two past participles: *got* and *gotten.* (The past participle is the form of a verb that's used with *have, had,* or *has.*) It's true that the British stopped using *have gotten* about three hundred years ago, while we in the Colonies kept using both *have got* and *have gotten.* But the result is not that Americans speak improper English. The result is that we have retained a nuance of meaning that the unfortunate Britons have lost.

When we say, *Fabio **has got** three Armani suits,* we mean he has them in his possession. It's another way of saying he *has* them.

When we say, *Fabio **has gotten** three Armani suits,* we mean he's acquired or obtained them.

It's a useful distinction, and one that the British would do well to reacquire.

TOMBSTONE: Drop the *of* in *all of* and *both of.*

R.I.P. Some members of the Redundancy Police think *of* is undesirable in the phrases *all of* and *both of,* except in front of a pronoun (*all of me, both of them,* etc.). They frown on sentences like *Both of the thieves spent all of the money,* and would prefer *Both the thieves spent all the money.*

Either way is correct. There's no law against keeping *of,* but by all means drop it if you want to. You can't please all of the people all the time. For more on dropping *of,* see page 132.

TOMBSTONE: Use *as . . . as* for positive comparisons, and *so . . . as* for negative ones. For example: *She's as old as Fran, but not so old as you.*

R.I.P. Not so fast! For centuries, it's been correct to use *as . . . as* in positive comparisons (*as fat as ever*) and to use either *as . . . as* or *so . . . as* in negative comparisons (*not as fat as before, not so fat as all that*). If you want to use *so . . . as* in a negative comparison, go right ahead. But *as . . . as* is correct in all cases.

If anyone tries to tell you otherwise, just remind him that in Old English, both *as* and *so* (*eall* and *swa*) appeared in the same word, *ealswa.* It was used in comparisons eight or more centuries ago pretty much the way we use *as* these days (*ealswa good ealswa gold*).

TOMBSTONE: Don't start a sentence with *there.*

R.I.P. There is no doubt that a statement starting with *there* begins on a weak note. It's weak because *there* is a phantom subject, standing in for the real one. *There is a party going on* is a different way of saying, *A party is going on.* The real subject in both cases is *party.*

Some English teachers frown on starting a sentence with *there*, possibly because they prefer keeping the real subject before the verb. Never mind. There's nothing wrong with it. In fact, literature is full of splendid examples: *"There is a tide in the affairs of men, which, taken at the flood, leads on to fortune."* There's more on pages 55 and 184.

Chapter 10

Saying Is Believing

How to Write What You Mean

A good writer is one you can read without breaking a sweat. If you want a workout, you don't lift a book—you lift weights. Yet we're brainwashed to believe that the more brilliant the writer, the tougher the going.

The truth is that the reader is always right. Chances are, if something you're reading doesn't make sense, it's not your fault—it's the writer's. And if something you write doesn't get your point across, it's probably not the reader's fault—it's yours. Too many readers are intimidated and humbled by what they can't understand, and in some cases that's precisely the effect the writer is after. But confusion is not complexity; it's just confusion. A venerable tradition, dating back to the ancient Greek orators, teaches that if you don't know what you're talking about, just ratchet up the level of difficulty and no one will ever know.

Don't confuse simplicity, though, with simplemindedness. A good writer can express an extremely complicated idea clearly and make the job look effortless. But such simplicity is a difficult thing to achieve, because to be clear in your writing you have to be clear in your thinking. This is why the simplest and clearest writing has the greatest power to delight, surprise, inform, and move the reader. You can't have this kind of shared understanding if writer and reader are in an adversary relationship.

Now, let's assume you know what you want to say, and the idea in your head is as clear as a mountain stream. (I'm allowed a cliché once in a while.) How can you avoid muddying it up when you put it into words?

There are no rules for graceful writing, at least not in the sense that there are rules for grammar and punctuation. Some writing manuals will tell you to write short sentences, or to cut out adjectives and adverbs. I disagree. The object isn't to simulate an android. When a sentence sounds nice, reads well, and is easy to follow, its length is just right. But when a sentence is lousy, you can take steps to make it more presentable. These are general principles, and you won't want to follow all of them all of the time (though it's not a bad idea).

1. Say what you have to say.

Unless you're standing at a lectern addressing an audience, there's no need to clear your throat. Your listeners aren't finding their seats, putting down their forks, wrapping up a conversation, or whatever. Your audience—the reader—is ready. So get to it.

These are the kinds of throat-clearing phrases you can usually ditch:

At this juncture I thought you might be interested in knowing . . .

Perhaps it would be valuable as we arrive at this point in time to recall . . .

I can assure you that I'm sincere when I say . . .

In light of recent developments the possibility exists that . . .

(Of course, some messages could do with a bit of cushioning: *We at the bank feel that under the circumstances you would want us to bring to your attention as soon as possible the fact that . . . your account is overdrawn.*)

2. Stop when you've said it.

Sometimes, especially when you're on a roll and coming up with your best stuff, it's hard to let go of a sentence (this one, for example), so when you get to the logical end you just keep going, and even though you know the reader's eyes are glazing over, you stretch one sentence thinner and thinner—with a semicolon here, a *however* or *nevertheless* there—and you end up stringing together a whole paragraph's worth of ideas before you finally realize it's all over and you're getting writer's cramp and you have to break down and use a period.

When it's time to start another sentence, start another sentence.

How do you know when it's time? Well, try breathing along with your sentences. Allow yourself one nice inhalation and exhalation per sentence as you silently read along. If you start to turn blue before getting to the end, either you're reading too slowly (don't move your lips) or the sentence is too long.

3. Don't belabor the obvious.

Some writers can't make a point without poking you in the ribs with it. A voice isn't just pleasing; it's pleasing *to the ear.* You don't just give something away; you give it away *for free.* The reader will get the point without the unnecessary prepositional phrases (phrases that start with words like *by, for, in, of,* and *to*): pretty *in appearance,* tall *of stature,* few *in number,* blue *in color,* small *in size,* stocky *in build,* plan *in advance,* drive *by car,* assemble *in a group.* You get the picture.

Speaking of redundancies, think twice before using expressions like *advance reservations, final conclusion, foreign import, free gift, prerecorded, refer back,* or *safe haven.* Do I hear an echo?

4. Don't tie yourself in knots to avoid repeating a word.

It's better to repeat a word that fits than to stick in a clumsy substitute that doesn't. Just because you've called something a spider once doesn't mean that the next time you have to call it an arachnid or a predaceous eight-legged creepy-crawly.

Editors sometimes call this attempt at elegant variation the Slender Yellow Fruit Syndrome. It is best explained by example: *Freddie was offered an apple and a banana, and he chose the slender yellow fruit.*

5. Be direct.

Too many writers back into what they have to say. A straightforward statement like *He didn't intend to ruin your flower bed* comes out *His intention was not to ruin your flower bed.*

Don't mince words. If what you mean is, *Mom reorganized my closet brilliantly,* don't water it down by saying, *Mom's reorganization of my closet was brilliant.*

Here are a couple of other examples:

Their house was destroyed in 1993. Not: *The destruction of their house occurred in 1993.*

We concluded that Roger's an idiot. Not: *Our conclusion was that Roger's an idiot.*

If you have something to say, be direct about it. As in geometry, the shortest distance between two points is a straight line.

6. Don't make yourself the center of the universe.

Of course we want to know what happened to you. Of course we care what you think and feel and do and say. But you can tell us without making every other word *I* or *me* or *my.* E-mailers are often guilty of this. Next time you write an e-mail or a letter (remember letters?), look it over and see how many sentences start with *I.*

You can prune phrases like *I think that,* or *in my opinion,* or *let me emphasize that* out of your writing (and your talking, for that matter) without losing anything. Anecdotes can be told, advice given, opinions opined, all with a lot fewer first-person pronouns than you think. ‹

This doesn't mean we don't love you.

7. Put descriptions close to what they describe.

A television journalist in the Farm Belt once said this about a suspected outbreak of hoof-and-mouth disease: *The pasture contained several cows seen by news reporters that were dead, diseased, or dying.*

Do you see what's wrong? The words *dead, diseased, or dying* are supposed to describe the cows, but they're so far from home that they seem to describe the reporters. What the journalist should have said was: *Reporters saw a pasture containing several cows that were dead, diseased, or dying.*

When a description strays too far, the sentence becomes awkward and hard to read. Here's an adjective (*bare*) that has strayed too far from the noun (*cupboard*) it describes: *Ms. Hubbard found her **cupboard**, although she'd gone shopping only a few hours before, **bare**.* Here's one way to rewrite it: *Although she'd gone shopping only a few hours before, Ms. Hubbard found her **cupboard bare**.*

And here's an adverb (*definitely*) that's strayed too far from its verb (*is suing*): *She **definitely**, if you can believe what all the papers are reporting and what everyone is saying, **is suing**.* Put them closer together: *She **definitely is suing**, if you can believe what all the papers are reporting and what everyone is saying.*

The reader shouldn't need a map to follow a sentence.

8. Put the doer closer to what's being done.

Nobody's saying that sentences can't be complex and interesting; they can, as long as they're easy to follow. But we shouldn't have to read a sentence twice to get it. Here's an example that takes us from Omaha to Sioux City by way of Pittsburgh:

*The **twins**, after stubbornly going to the same high school despite the advice of their parents and teachers, **chose** different colleges.*

Find a way to say it that puts the doer (the subject, *twins*) closer to what's being done (the verb, *chose*): *The **twins chose** different colleges, after stubbornly going to the same high school despite the advice of their parents and teachers.*

If you need a compass to navigate a sentence, take another whack at the writing.

9. Watch out for pronounitis.

A sentence with too many pronouns (*he, him, she, her, it, they, them,* and other words that substitute for nouns) can give your reader hives: *Fleur says Judy told **her** boyfriend about **their** stupid little adventure and **she** already regrets **it**.*

Whose boyfriend? Whose stupid little adventure? Who regrets what?

When you write things like this, of course you know the cast of characters. It won't be so clear to somebody else. Don't make the reader guess. Here's a possibility: *Judy told her boyfriend about her stupid little adventure with Fleur and already regrets telling him, according to Fleur.*

10. Make sure there's a time and place for everything.

Mr. Big's administrative assistant got a raise by hinting that she'd found a candid photo of him and Natasha in a compromising position in the file cabinet during Administrative Professionals Week.

What happened in the file cabinet? And when? Did the shenanigans take place during Administrative Professionals Week? Or is that when the administrative assistant put the squeeze on Mr. Big? This calls for some administrative assistance.

Mr. Big's administrative assistant got a raise by hinting during Administrative Professionals Week that she'd found in the file cabinet a candid photo of him and Natasha in a compromising position.

Where are we? What's going on? What time is it? These are questions the reader shouldn't have to ask.

11. Imagine what you're writing.
Picture in your mind any images you've created.

Are they unintentionally funny, like this one? *The bereaved family covered the mirrors as a reflection of its grief.* If you don't see what's wrong, reflect on it for a moment.

Are there too many images, as in this sentence? *The remaining bone of contention is a thorn in his side and an albatross around his neck.* Give the poor guy a break. One image at a time, please.

12. Put your ideas in order.

Don't make the reader rearrange your messy sentences to figure out what's going on. The parts should follow logically. This doesn't mean they should be rattled off in chronological order, but the sequence of ideas should make sense. Here's how Gracie Allen might have talked about a soufflé recipe, for instance:

It is possible to make this soufflé with four eggs instead of eight. But it will collapse and possibly even catch fire in the oven, leaving you with a flat, burned soufflé. Now, you wouldn't want that, would you? So if you have only four eggs, reduce all the other ingredients in the recipe by half.

Rearrange the ideas:

This soufflé recipe calls for eight eggs. If you want to use fewer, reduce the other ingredients accordingly. If the proportions aren't maintained, the soufflé could flatten or burn.

13. Get the big picture.

Forget the details for a minute. Now step back and take a look at what you've written. Have you said what you wanted to say? After all, leaving the wrong impression is much worse than making a couple of grammatical boo-boos. Get some perspective.

Assuming you've made your point, ask yourself whether you could make it more smoothly. Somebody once said that in good writing, the sentences hold hands. See if you can give yours a helping hand. It may be that by adding or subtracting a word here or there, you could be even clearer. Or you could switch two sentences around, or begin one of them differently.

14. Read with a felonious mind.

There's no easy way to raise your writing from competence to artistry. It helps, though, to read with a felonious mind. If you see a letter or memo or report that you admire, read it again. Why do you like it, and what makes it so effective? When you find a technique that works, steal it. Someday, others may be stealing from you.

Chapter 11

E-Mail Intuition

Does Anything Go?

And now, a word to the wired: E-mail is no excuse for lousy English.

Granted, virtual writing is usually more informal than writing in the "real" world. But informal doesn't mean incoherent—or it shouldn't. Unfortunately, much of the writing you see in cyberspace (and e-mail isn't the only culprit) barely qualifies as English. The words are chosen with little or no thought. The grammar is a mess. The punctuation is either absent or in your face. As for spelling, it's hit-or-miss—usually miss. No wonder the whole point of an e-mail is often lost in transmission.

Don't bother rounding up the usual suspects. Even people who are normally careful about their English may throw the rules out the window when they go online. Maybe they don't think of e-mail as writing. Maybe they don't realize that good English is just as important online as off.

In fact, misunderstandings are more likely in an e-mail than in a letter or a phone call or a face-to-face conversation. The speed, the brevity, the disengagement of online writing all conspire to muddle your message. And the short attention span of the wired reader only makes things worse.

What's more, the virtual world is full of strangers, people who know you only by your words. Sure, your best friend will overlook a few misspellings or lapses in grammar. But people you've never met will judge you solely by what they see on their computer screens. To them, you are what you write.

In short, online writing needs all the help it can get. Good English is clear English. It's efficient, precise, sensible, economical, sometimes even beautiful. And that's just as true in e-mail as it is in snail mail—or any other kind of writing.

E-mail that's hard to understand—ambiguous, poorly worded, misspelled, unpunctuated—takes only an instant to send but forever to decipher. So e-mail unto others as you would have them e-mail unto you.

That means you don't call time-out when you log on. Such niceties as grammar, spelling, and punctuation *do* matter online, plus a few more besides. Here are some things for the wired writer to consider before clicking Send.

The Right Connection

How finicky are you about e-mail? Most people I know think of it as a new species, a cross between a phone call and a letter. Those who see it more like a letter are pickier about the fine points. The free-spirited types treat it more like a phone call and don't sweat the details.

Who's right? Both factions, some of the time. The issue isn't e-mail itself, but the person who's getting it. If you're e-mailing your English professor, for example, you'd better be letter perfect. But if you're messaging your flaky little brother, loosen up.

The point is, the audience should be your guide. That means customizing your e-mail—the vocabulary, the level of formality, the mood, the sophistication, the humor—to fit the reader.

So when you message the prof, keep it straight: *I don't understand the essay question on postmodernism.* When you e-mail little bro, go for it: *Say what?*

Subject Matter

You'd never know it by looking at the queue of unread messages in the typical in-box, but the subject line can make or break an e-mail.

The subject line determines how soon a message is read—if at all. Yet many e-mailers kiss it off and some don't even bother filling it in. What's the poor reader to make of a pointless subject line like *Hmmm* or *FYI* or *Stuff* or, worst of all, *<no subject>*?

If you'd like your e-mail read before it grows mold, here's some friendly advice on the subject.

- Be specific. Don't make readers guess what your message is about. Instead of saying *The project* or *A meeting,* give them a clue: *Opie's science project* or *Otis's AA meeting.*
- Don't cry wolf. If your message can wait, say so: *Query for Leonard—no rush.* On the other hand, if it's urgent, speak up: *Virginia: Need reply by noon.* But don't wear out the panic button if you want it to work when you really need it.
- Watch the spelling. A subject line is the last place you want a spelling (or grammar or punctuation) error to creep in. Why should the reader bother with your message when you obviously didn't?
- Hold the hype. Any hint of spam in the subject line, particularly if the reader isn't familiar with your e-mail address, can be the kiss of death. Nobody likes junk mail. If you're e-mailing Ben & Jerry's with an idea for a new ice cream flavor, for example, skip the hard sell (*This is your lucky day*) and say it straight (*Caramel Miranda*).

Imprint this on your noodle: The object of the subject is to inform the reader.

Screen Test

Imagine that Aunt Dahlia sends Bertie an e-mail about her plans to take a two-week tour of Tibet. After reading several screenfuls about a lamasery on the slopes of Mount Guopei, Bertie stores the message to finish later. Before he gets around to it, Aunt Dahlia is on his doorstep with her three favorite foxhounds and a fortnight's supply of kibble.

Yes, Bertie should have read the whole message. But Aunt Dahlia should have mentioned the dog-sitting job up front and saved the colorful travelogue for later.

As I've said before, wired readers have short attention spans. If you have something important to tell them, say it somewhere in the first screenful. What's less important can go later, but don't rattle on indefinitely. You're writing an e-mail, not the *Encyclopaedia Britannica.*

The computer makes it easy to go on and on and on. You empty all your ideas into the word processor. If you can't decide which ones are best, you keep them all. When you run out of ideas, you cut and paste someone else's. Isn't technology wonderful?

Well, not so wonderful when you're on the receiving end. Everyone knows that long messages are the ones that get read last. So be selective. It's easier to dump in everything, but resist the urge. (If you need help with the pruning, see Chapter 10.)

Getting to Know You

Call me old-fashioned, but I find it jarring to get an e-mail without a hello or a good-bye. Cyberia is chilly enough already. Why not warm things up with a greeting and a closing?

You don't have to be stiff or starchy about it. Most of the time, a simple *Hi, Alice* and *Bye, Trixie* will do. But keep it more formal when your message really matters—say, in an e-mail to the prospective boss of your dreams.

An e-mail without a salutation or a signature can seem abrupt and impersonal, even rude. It's like a phone call from someone who starts talking with no preliminaries, then hangs up without saying good-bye.

Politeness aside, there are other reasons for using a greeting and a closing. Perhaps you're writing to someone who shares an e-mail address with somebody else. Or maybe you share one yourself. Why leave any question about who's getting the message or who's sending it? Then again, you might be messaging people who don't recognize your address. Why make them puzzle it out?

Yes, you're in a hurry when you write e-mail. But it takes

only seconds to add a *Yo, Phoebe* and a *See ya, Holden*. And what a difference they make!

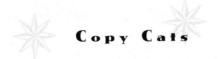

Copy Cats

In the old typewriter days, making copies was a hassle (remember carbon paper?). Nowadays copying is a snap. With a few clicks, you can send copies or forwards or attachments to everybody in your address book. The down side of all this wizardry is that the average in-basket is as stuffed as a Thanksgiving turkey.

Do you need to cc everybody in the book club that you'll be late Wednesday night? Should you send the boss an attachment every time you submit a report to a client? Must you forward that list of lightbulb jokes to everyone in your organic chemistry class? I think not.

If Uncle Fred really needs to see your e-mail to cousin Bamm-Bamm, by all means send him a copy. But if he doesn't need the whole thing, cut and paste just the part he has to see, and send it in a separate e-mail.

Do your bit to fight clutter. Don't copy or forward or attach something just because you can.

Type Dreams

The only thing more annoying than an unnecessary e-mail is an unreadable one—something you can't read without getting eyestrain. You know the kind: a message that's all UPPER-CASE or lowercase, especially one with no punctuation or paragraph breaks.

Hard-to-read messages do serve a purpose. By forcing us to squint at our computer screens, they keep things hopping at the optometrist's. And I'll bet all that peering with furrowed brow helps sell a lot of acetaminophen and wrinkle cream.

Headaches and wrinkles aside, punctuation and paragraph breaks and occasional capital letters are handy signals to the reader. They show where sentences begin and end, where the subject changes, and where people and places and dates come into the picture. Nobody likes to stare at an unbroken blob of indistinguishable type.

In addition to the vision thing, a lot of people think an e-mailer who uses all caps is SHOUTING. So turn down the volume.

Jargonistas

IMHO (in my humble opinion), those abbreviations that worm their way into online writing—like CUL (see you later) and BTW (by the way)—are juvenile and irritating. So are those little smileys and frownies made of punctuation marks that are supposed to show how the writer feels. Come on, kids. Aren't punctuation marks abused enough already? :-(

That stuff reminds me of grade school and secret handshakes. You may disagree, of course. A lot of reasonable people do. But I'd rather use words.

If you feel you must use a cutesy abbreviation or emoticon to save a few words or express an emotion, go ahead. Just make sure the reader understands your slanguage. An analog soul—and there are still a lot of us out there—might not get it.

Oh, I see. You're too busy to write complete sentences. So what are you doing with the time you save by using clever shortcuts? Volunteering at the homeless shelter? Delivering Meals on Wheels? Sure you are. I'm ROFL—rolling on floor laughing. :-)

Response Ability

Say Mr. Kane sends out a few hundred e-mails on a few hundred subjects to a few hundred people in the course of a month. Now let's say he gets back a few hundred replies along the lines of *That's possible* or *OK* or *Not just yet* or *I'll think it over.* Come again? Information please!

A cryptic reply won't do the job when you're answering a busy citizen like Mr. K., especially if a lot of time has passed or if the subject line is no help. The last thing he wants to do is slog through his outgoing mail to remind himself what he asked you.

Don't give the reader a hard time. Be clear about what you're replying to. Either sum up the original e-mail in a few words (*About your request for a potted palm in the lobby* . . .), or cut and paste the relevant parts. There's usually no need to quote the whole thing.

You can also do the summarizing in the subject line. If the one that pops up when you click Reply is too vague (*Re: A request*), rewrite it: *Your request for a potted palm.*

Spellbound

A spell-checker can be your best friend—and your worst enemy.

I use mine all the time, and I can't count the times it's saved my bacon. For example, I'm incapable of typing the word *substitution* correctly. My fingers simply can't do it. If it weren't for my speller, I'd have to use *replacement* or *stand-in* or *pinch hitter* instead.

I also tend to misspell *the*—it comes out *hte*. Or I write it twice: *the the*. Spell-check bails me out every time.

But the good old speller doesn't always come through. Turn your back on it, and it'll kick you in the but. There! That's what I mean. My software didn't catch that *but* because it can't tell the different between sound-alike words: *but* and *butt*, *need* and *knead*, *sew* and *sow*, and so on.

Word processors may have dictionaries, but they don't have common sense—at least not yet. The lesson? Use your spell-checker, but don't follow it blindly. Don't automatically hit Replace every time the program tells you to. Yule bee sari!

As for your so-called grammar-checker, forget about it. Most of the "mistakes" it finds aren't mistakes at all, and much of the advice comes from the Twilight Zone. The other day, I wrote an e-mail with the phrase "an hour-long program" and ran my grammar checker just for the heck of it. I was told to change *an* to *a*. No, I did not hit Replace. (For the inside story on *a* and *an*, see page 131.)

Repeat Performance

If you haven't given your e-mail a second look, you're not ready to click Send.

I know what you're thinking: *It's only an e-mail. Getting it out is more important than getting it perfect.* Well, just because an e-mail travels instantly doesn't mean you have to send it instantly.

Sure you're busy. But your reader doesn't have all day, either. The time you save by not rereading an e-mail is time the other guy has to spend deciphering it. And what about all the time you'll spend clearing up what should have been clear the first time?

In other words, rereading isn't a time waster, it's a time saver. Think of it as preventive maintenance. With a little regular servicing, you can avoid lengthy visits to the repair shop to overhaul your e-mail clunkers.

A Civil Tongue

E-mail can turn the nicest person into a tactless lout. It's the nature of the medium. Unlike a phone call or an in-the-flesh conversation, an electronic message lacks the vocal nuances, the give-and-take, the body English that do so much to soften the sharp edges of a poorly chosen word.

Here on earth, a smile, a murmur, a nod, a chuckle can do the job of a missing courtesy like "May I?" or "Excuse me." But in cyberspace, words have to stand alone, unless you count such inadequate crutches as smileys and abbreviations.

Of course, words have to stand alone on paper too, but writing a "real" letter is a slower, more leisurely process, especially if you're using pen and ink. You're more careful, for one thing. If you flub the penmanship or word choice, you'll have to wad up the page and start over. And built-in delays like addressing the envelope, finding a stamp, and getting to the mailbox give you time to reconsider and avoid thoughtless blunders.

All in all, it's easier to inadvertently hurt someone's feelings in an e-mail than in a letter, a phone call, or a face-to-face talk. A casual comment or a brusque remark that would pass harmlessly at the water cooler, for instance, might touch off World War III in an e-mail.

Next time you log on and enter the ozone, don't check your manners at the portal. Here's what to do instead:

- Dust off a few Old World expressions like "please," "thank you," and "I'm sorry." There's no law against being nice online.
- Go for the extra word or two if that will make you clearer. Why be stingy, especially when you're dealing with a sensitive topic?
- Don't click Send when your blood is boiling. Try clicking Send Later and waiting for your temperature to drop to 98.6.

- Get real and ask yourself whether a phone call, a letter, or a "live" meeting would be better. One brief conversation might do the job of a dozen e-mails. And a letter might be more appropriate if you're thanking Great-Aunt Betsey for her generous graduation present.
- Be discreet about what you send and to whom, especially at work. E-mail isn't the place for sensitive personnel matters, criticism of third parties, office romance, hurtful gossip, or anything else that could find its way to the wrong mailbox.

So don't let e-mail bring out the beast in you. If you feel yourself growing fangs and sprouting hair from the backs of your hands, get a grip. You're a real person writing to real people. Yes, even in the virtual world.

Glossary

ADJECTIVE. A word describing or characterizing a noun. It can come before the noun (*pink sweater*) or after (*The sweater is pink*). Because an adjective adds something to a noun, it's called a modifier; we say it "modifies" the noun.

ADVERB. A word that describes or characterizes a verb (*He grunted lugubriously*). It can also characterize an adjective (*He is very lugubrious*) or another adverb (*He grunted very lugubriously*). An adverb is called a modifier, because it "modifies" another word.

APOSTROPHE. A mark of punctuation that's used to make nouns possessive (*Albert's coat*), to form some plurals (*the 1950's*), and to show where letters have been omitted, as in contractions (*wouldn't*).

ARTICLE. The three articles (*a, an, the*) are actually tiny adjectives that tell us whether a noun refers to a particular thing (*the* chair, *the* ottoman) or just one of those things (*a* chair, *an* ottoman). *The* is called the definite article; *a* and *an* are indefinite articles.

BRACKETS. Marks of punctuation used in quoted material or excerpts to enclose something that's not part of the original, like an explanatory aside. *"My weight [154 pounds] is a well-kept secret," said Leona.*

CLAUSE. A group of words with its own subject and verb. A simple sentence might consist of only one clause: *Ernest left for Paris.* More complex sentences have several clauses, as in this example: *I learned | that Ernest left for Paris | when Scott told me.* Independent clauses make sense alone (*I put on a sock . . .*), but dependent, or subordinate, clauses don't (*. . . that had no mate*).

CLICHÉ. A figure of speech that's lost its sparkle. When you find yourself using one, nip it in the bud—or maybe I should put that another way.

COLLECTIVE NOUN. A noun that stands for a group of people or things, like *total* or *number.* It can be considered singular (*The **number** is staggering*) or plural (*A **number** of them have gone their separate ways*).

COLON. A punctuation mark that can be used to introduce a statement, a series of things, a quotation, or instructions. It's a pause in the traffic, telling you to brake before going on.

COMMA. A punctuation mark that indicates a pause. If it were a traffic signal, it would be a yellow light. It can be used to separate clauses in a sentence, or items in a series.

CONDITIONAL CLAUSE. A clause that starts with *if, as if, as though,* or some other expression of supposition. The verb in a conditional clause has an attitude: that is, it takes on different forms, or "moods," depending on the speaker's attitude or intention toward what's being said. When the clause states a condition that's contrary to fact, the verb is in the subjunctive mood (*If I **were** you . . .*). When the clause states a condition that may be true, the verb is in the indicative mood (*If I **was** late . . .*). For more on the conditional, see VERB.

CONJUNCTION. A connecting word. The telltale part of this term is "junction," because that's where a conjunction is found—at the junction where words or phrases or clauses or sentences are joined. The most familiar conjunctions are *and, but,* and *or.* And it's fine to start a sentence with one. But not too often. Or you'll overdo it.

CONSONANT. Generally, a letter with a "hard" sound: *b, c, d, f, g, h, j, k, l, m, n, p, q, r, s, t, v, w, x, y, z.* Sometimes the consonants *w* and *y* act like vowels, which are letters with a "soft," openmouthed sound. And occasionally consonants (such as *g, h,* and others) are seen but not heard.

CONTRACTION. Two words combined into one, with an apostrophe showing where letters are omitted. There are three kinds of contractions: a verb plus *not* (*do + not = don't*); a pronoun plus a verb (*they + are = they're*); and a noun plus a verb (*Bob + is = Bob's*). Don't confuse the last example with the possessive (*Bob's dog*).

DANGLER. A word or phrase in the wrong place that ends up describing the wrong thing: *After napping, the card table was set up.* Who was napping? Unless it's the table, change the sentence: *After napping, Oscar set up the card table.*

DASH. A punctuation mark that interrupts a sentence to insert another thought. One can act like a colon: *It was every mother's nightmare—ringworm.* Or a pair of dashes can be used like parentheses: *The remedy was easy enough—a simple oral medication—but what would she tell the neighbors?*

DICTIONARY. A book that lists words in alphabetical order and gives their spellings and pronunciations, their meanings and origins—including words that aren't legit, like *alright*. The fact that a word can be found in the dictionary doesn't mean it's all right. Read the fine print.

DOUBLE NEGATIVE. A double negative is what you get when you combine a negative verb (like *have not* or *is not*) with a negative pronoun (like *nothing* or *nobody*), a negative adverb (like *hardly* or *never*), or a negative conjunction (like *neither* or *nor*). Not all double negatives are no-nos. Here are some flagrant examples of don'ts: *I have not seen nobody. It wasn't hardly worth it. He is not there, neither.* Some allowables: *It's not inconceivable. She's not unappealing.*

ELLIPSIS POINTS. Punctuation that indicates an omission, or ellipsis, in a quotation. The three dots can show the omission of a word—in this case a naughty one: *"Get off my lawn, and take your . . . dog with you!" he shouted.* Or they can show where a sentence trails off: *"Now let me think. . . ."* Notice that when the ellipsis points come at the end of the sentence, a period precedes them, so you end up with four dots instead of three. (If you want to emphasize the incompleteness of the trailing off, you may end with a space, then just three dots: "But . . .")

EXCLAMATION POINT. A punctuation mark that comes after something that's exclaimed: *"I passed!" said Pippa.* Go easy on the exclamation point and save it for the really startling stuff.

FIGURATIVE. Language is figurative when it uses words in imaginative or out-of-the-ordinary ways. In the process, the truth is often stretched to make a point. If you were being literal, you might say: *Jack's dog is big and stocky.* But to be more vivid, you could say: *Jack's dog is built like a refrigerator.*

FIGURE OF SPEECH. An imaginative (or "figurative") expression: *She knows how to push his buttons.* (See FIGURATIVE.) When a figure of speech gets stale, it becomes a cliché.

GERUND. A word that's made of a verb plus *ing* (*bowling*, for example) and that acts as a noun: ***Bowling** is his first love.* The same *ing* word is a participle if it acts as an adjective (*He's a **bowling** fool*) or part of a verb (*He was **bowling***).

GRAMMAR. A system of rules for arranging words into sentences. We adopt rules when we need them and discard them when we don't, so the rules are always changing.

HYPHEN. A mark of punctuation that looks like a stubby dash. It is used to join words together to make new ones (*self-conscious*), and to link syllables when a word, like *humongous* here, breaks off at the end of a line and continues on the next.

IMPERATIVE. A verb is imperative when the speaker is expressing a command or request: *Lose twenty pounds, Jack.* (See MOOD.)

INDICATIVE. A verb is indicative when the speaker is expressing a straightforward statement or question: *Jack **lost** twenty pounds.* (See MOOD.)

INFINITIVE. A verb in its simplest form (*sneeze,* for example). While the preposition *to* is usually a signal that the infinitive is being used (*to sneeze*), it's not part of the infinitive itself. Putting an adverb in the middle (*to loudly sneeze*) is fine—you're not really "splitting" anything.

INTERJECTION. A word (or words) expressing a sudden rush of feeling: *My word! Help! Wow! Oh, damn!*

INTERROGATIVE. An expression is interrogative if it asks a question: *Got that?*

INTRANSITIVE. See VERB.

JARGON. Language used by windbags and full of largely meaningless, pseudotechnical terms that are supposed to lend the speaker an aura of expertise. The advantage of jargon is that you can use it to discuss things you know little about, and without really saying anything. But even when you know what you're talking about, technical language can be confusing to someone who isn't another expert. *Jargon* comes from an old word for "chattering" or "twittering."

LITERAL. True or "to the letter"—the opposite of figurative. Don't use the adverb *literally* to modify a figure of speech, as in: *The boss literally had kittens.*

METAPHOR. The most common figure of speech. A metaphor takes the language normally used for one thing and applies it to something else: *His stomach began to growl. The moon was a silver coin upon the water.*

Mood. Verbs have attitude. They take on different forms, called *moods,* or sometimes *modes,* that reflect the speaker's attitude toward what's being said. There are three moods in English. If what's being said is an ordinary statement or question about facts, the verb is in the indicative mood. (*He is on my foot.*) If what's being said is contrary to fact or expresses a wish, the verb is in the subjunctive mood. (*I wish he were not on my foot. If he were not on my foot, I could go.*) If what's being said is a command or a request, the verb is in the imperative mood. (*Get off my foot!*)

Noun. A word that stands for a person, place, thing, or idea. A common noun starts with a small letter (*city* or *girl* or *religion,* for example); a proper noun starts with a capital letter (*Memphis* or *Molly* or *Methodist*).

Object. A noun or pronoun that's acted on by a verb. It can be something you give, for instance, or somebody you give it to. An indirect object is the person or thing on the receiving end of the action, and a direct object is who or what ends up there: *Harry gave me* [indirect object] *the flu* [direct object]. Think of it like a game of catch—you throw a direct object to an indirect object.

Additionally, a noun or pronoun at the receiving end of a preposition (*to* and *from* in these examples) is an object: *Harry gave the flu to me. He is from Chicago.*

Parentheses. Marks of punctuation used to enclose an aside—either a whole sentence or words within a sentence.

PARTS OF SPEECH. The eight kinds of words: noun, pronoun, adjective, verb, adverb, preposition, conjunction, interjection. This sentence uses all of them: *But* [conjunction] *gosh* [interjection], *you* [pronoun] *are* [verb] *really* [adverb] *in* [preposition] *terrible* [adjective] *trouble* [noun]!

PERIOD. A punctuation mark that shows where a declarative sentence, one that states something, ends. The period is also used in some abbreviations (U.S. for "United States," Dr. for "Doctor," P.M. for "post meridiem"), but many abbreviations have dropped their dots.

PHRASE. A group of related words without subject and verb, like *glorious sunset* or *in the meantime* or *to spill the beans* or *gently swinging in the breeze*. A group of words with both a subject and its verb is a clause.

PLURAL. More than one; just one is singular. Plural nouns generally have endings different from singular ones (*berries* versus *berry*, for example).

POSSESSIVE. Showing ownership. With most nouns, you get the possessive form (or "case") by adding 's (*Alice's cousin*) or the preposition *of* (*a cousin of Alice*). A "double possessive" uses both methods (*a cousin of Alice's*).

PREPOSITION. A word that "positions" or situates words in relation to one another. The roots of the term *preposition* mean "put before," which is appropriate, because a preposition usually comes before a noun or pronoun: *My cousin is from Philly.* (Contrary to what you might have heard, however, it can indeed go at the end of a sentence.) The prepositions we use most are *about, above, across, after, against, ahead*

of, along, among, around, as, at, away from, before, behind, be-
low, beneath, beside, between, but (in the sense of "except"),
by, down, except, for, from, in, in back of, in front of, inside,
into, like, of, off, on, onto, out, out of, outside, over, past, since,
through, throughout, to, toward, under, until, up, upon, with,
within, without. Some of these words can serve as other parts
of speech as well (adverbs, conjunctions).

PRONOUN. A word that can be used in place of a noun.
Pronouns fall into these categories:

- A **personal pronoun** can be a subject (*I, you, he, she,*
  it, we, they); an object (*me, you, him, her, it, us, them*); or
  a possessive (*my, mine, your, yours, his, her, hers, its, our,*
  ours, their, theirs). Some of these (*my, your, his, her, its,*
  our, their) are also called possessive adjectives, since
  they describe (or modify) nouns.

- A **reflexive pronoun** calls attention to itself (it ends
  with *self* or *selves*): *myself, yourself, himself, herself, itself,*
  ourselves, yourselves, themselves. Reflexive pronouns are
  used to emphasize (*She **herself** is Hungarian*) or to refer
  to the subject (*He blames **himself***).

- A **demonstrative pronoun** points out something:
  this, that, these, those. It can be used by itself (*Hold **this***)
  or with a noun, as an adjective (*Who is **this** guy?*).

- An **indefinite pronoun** refers to a vague or unknown
  person or thing: *all, another, any, anybody, anyone, any-*
  thing, both, each, either, every, everybody, everyone, every-
  thing, few, many, much, neither, no one, nobody, none,
  one, other, several, some, somebody, someone, something,

such (**All** *is lost*). Some of these, too, can serve as adjectives.

- An **interrogative pronoun** is used to ask a question: *what, which, who, whom, whose* (**Who's** *on first?*).

- A **relative pronoun** introduces a dependent (or subordinate) clause: *that, what, whatever, which, whichever, who, whoever, whom, whomever, whose* (*He's the guy* **who** *stole my heart*).

PUNCTUATION. The signs and signals in writing that direct the traffic of language. They call for stops, starts, slowdowns, and detours. The marks of punctuation include the period, the comma, the colon, the semicolon, the question mark, the exclamation point, the apostrophe, the dash, the hyphen, parentheses, ellipsis points, and quotation marks.

QUESTION MARK. A punctuation mark that comes at the end of a question.

QUOTATION MARKS. Punctuation marks that surround spoken or quoted words.

SEMICOLON. A punctuation mark for a stop that's less final than a period. It's like a flashing red light—it lets you drive on after a brief pause. You'll often find it between clauses in a sentence and between items in a series.

SENTENCE. A word or group of words that expresses a complete thought; in writing, it begins with a capital letter and has a concluding mark like a period, a question mark, or an exclamation point. Most sentences have a subject and a verb, but not all. An imperative sentence, which demands an action, may have only a verb (*Run!*). An interrogative sentence, which asks a question, may also have only one word (*How?*). An exclamatory sentence, which expresses emotion, may have only a word or a phrase (*Good heavens!*). The declarative sentence, the most common kind, conveys information and is likely to have a subject, a verb, and an object—usually in that order: *He ate my fries.*

SIBILANT. A consonant sound that hisses, like *s, z, sh, zh, ch,* and *j.* Nouns that end in sibilants sometimes have special ways of forming plurals and possessives.

SINGULAR. Only one; more than one is plural. A noun or a verb is singular if it applies to a single person, place, or thing.

STUFFED SHIRT. A person likely to use jargon; similar to a windbag. (See JARGON.)

SUBJECT. That which initiates an action; in other words, who or what is doing whatever's being done. Subjects can be nouns (like *Harry*), pronouns (like *I*), or phrases (like *Harry and I*). *Good old **Harry and I** have fallen arches.* A subject with all its accessories (*Good old Harry and I*) is the complete subject. One stripped to its bare essentials (*Harry and I*) is the simple or basic subject.

SUBJUNCTIVE. A verb is in the subjunctive (see MOOD) when the intention is to express:

1. A wish (*I wish Jack **were** here*).

2. A conditional (*if*) statement that's contrary to fact (*If Jack **were** here . . .*).

3. A suggestion or demand (*We insist that Jack **be** here*).

SYLLABLE. Part of a word that is pronounced as a single unit. The word *syllable* has three syllables: SIL-la-bul. *Word* is a one-syllable word.

TENSE. What a verb uses to tell time. The basic tenses—present, past, future—and the variations on them tell us when an action takes place, took place, will take place, and so on. We're always telling time with verbs, since whenever we use one, there's a "when" built in. See VERB for examples of some common verb forms at work.

TRANSITIVE. See VERB.

VERB. An action word. In a sentence, it tells you what's going on: *She **sells** seashells.* Verbs are called transitive when they need an object to make sense (*Henry **raises** dahlias*) and intransitive when they make sense without one (*Flowers **die***). Also see MOOD and TENSE.

Here's what some common verb forms look like, for the first person singular (*I*) and the verb *eat*.

	PRESENT	PAST	FUTURE	CONDITIONAL
SIMPLE	I eat	I ate	I will eat	I would eat
PROGRESSIVE	I am eating	I was eating	I will be eating	I would be eating
PERFECT	I have eaten	I had eaten	I will have eaten	I would have eaten

VOWEL. A letter with a "soft," openmouthed sound: *a, e, i, o, u*. The other letters are consonants; two of them, *w* and *y*, sometimes act like vowels. (*Few boys own many cows.*)

Bibliography

Here are some books you may find helpful, including many that I turn to again and again. (A dictionary isn't optional, though. It's required.)

The Careful Writer: A Modern Guide to English Usage. Theodore M. Bernstein. New York: The Free Press, 1995.

A Dictionary of Contemporary American Usage. Bergen Evans and Cornelia Evans. New York: Random House, 1957.

A Dictionary of Modern American Usage. Bryan A. Garner. New York: Oxford University Press, 1998.

A Dictionary of Modern English Usage. H. W. Fowler. 2nd ed., revised by Ernest Gowers. New York: Oxford University Press, 1983.

The Elements of Style. William Strunk, Jr., and E. B. White. 3rd ed. New York: Macmillan, 1979.

Essentials of English Grammar. Otto Jespersen. Tuscaloosa: University of Alabama Press, 1964.

Harper's English Grammar. John B. Opdycke. Revised ed. New York: Warner Books, 1991.

The Language Instinct. Steven Pinker. New York: Harper Perennial, 2000.

Modern American Usage: A Guide. Wilson Follett. Edited and completed by Jacques Barzun et al. New York: Hill & Wang, 1966.

The New York Public Library Writer's Guide to Style and Usage. Edited by Andrea J. Sutcliffe. New York: HarperCollins, 1994.

Plain Words: Their ABC. Ernest Gowers. New York: Knopf, 1954.

Simple & Direct: A Rhetoric for Writers. Jacques Barzun. Revised ed. Chicago: University of Chicago Press, 1994.

Style: Toward Clarity and Grace. Joseph M. Williams. Chicago: University of Chicago Press, 1995.

Words Fail Me: What Everyone Who Writes Should Know About Writing. Patricia T. O'Conner. San Diego: Harvest, 1999.

Words into Type. Marjorie E. Skillin, Robert M. Gay, et al. 3rd ed. Englewood Cliffs, NJ: Prentice-Hall, 1974.

You Send Me: Getting It Right When You Write Online. Patricia T. O'Conner and Stewart Kellerman. New York: Harcourt, 2002.

DICTIONARIES

The American Heritage Dictionary of the English Language. 4th ed. Boston: Houghton Mifflin, 2000.

Webster's New World College Dictionary. 4th ed. New York: John Wiley & Sons, 1999.

Note: If you spend a lot of time on the computer, consider getting a CD-ROM dictionary. When you're busy, the answer is just a click away. *The New Oxford American Dictionary,* published by Oxford University Press, is a good choice.

Index